THE PILGRIM CONTINUES HIS WAY

THE
PILGRIM CONTINUES
HIS WAY

Translated from the Russian by

R. M. FRENCH

Triangle, SPCK
Holy Trinity Church
Marylebone Road
London NW1 4DU

First published by SPCK 1943
also with *The Way of a Pilgrim*
New edition, with *The Way of a Pilgrim*, 1954
Paperback edition 1973
Fifth impression 1982
First Triangle edition 1986

British Library Cataloguing in Publication Data

The pilgrim continues his way.—5th ed.
 1. Russka i a pravoslavna i a t serkov
 2. Christian life   3. Prayer
 I. French, R. M.   II. Iz razskazov strannika o
blagodatnam dieĭstviĭ nolitvy Iisusovoĭ. *English*
 248.3'2   BX382

 ISBN 0-281-04238-1

Reproduced, printed and bound in Great Britain by
Hazell Watson & Viney Limited,
Member of the BPCC Group,
Aylesbury, Bucks

Preface

I HOPE those who know this Russian Pilgrim will be glad to meet him again and spend a little more time in his company.

When I turned *The Way of a Pilgrim* into English some ten years or so ago I had no idea that this continuation existed. It came into my hands, however, not very long afterwards. But a natural mistrust of sequels, second parts and the like made me doubtful of the wisdom of translating it. Further thought, and the continuous welcome given to the first part, have led me to change my mind. So here the second part is. It has almost as little framework as the first. The Pilgrim appears almost as abruptly as when we met him first, and in a sense he does not make an exit at all. He and his friends just stop talking. The book is made up of three more sections, to add to the four in Part I. The first is narrative, the other two contain a discussion about prayer, in which some things are said which sound strange in Western ears.

I feel little doubt that this really is a continuation and that it was written by the same hand. Or, at least, I feel sure that the first and narrative section was. It has the authentic ring, the same charm and naïveté. But it is a little difficult to suppose that the Pilgrim himself is responsible for recording the long-drawn-out and at times technical discussion of prayer in the latter part of the book. It hardly fits in with our impression of his mind, or, indeed, with what he tells us about himself. But it is to be noted that these two sections are not, as the others were, reported to his spiritual father. The discussions take place in the latter's presence—in fact, it is he who organizes them. Perhaps someone at some time added the last two sections to the Pilgrim's five narratives.

To be perfectly frank, it was the literary charm of the Pilgrim's narrative which first led me to give it an English dress. But in doing so I soon came to recognize its value from a spiritual point of view. That value lies in something more than its advocacy of a particular method of prayer. That method is, I think, *pace* the Skhimnik, not everybody's method after all. In any case it should be carefully noted that the Hermit himself insists upon the great importance of having the continuous guidance of a "wise and experienced director."

But the book is saturated with the sense of the Presence of God. The spiritual experience it portrays is simple, direct, full of charity and joy. It is dominated by the thought of the happiness and strength which come to a human life which tries to keep in close touch with God. Many who cannot attain to the automatic prayer of the heart may yet learn to look back upon a day, a year, a life, and say, "I walked along with the Prayer," even if at times "the Prayer went with difficulty."

I have added two rough sketch-maps which show the places which the Pilgrim visited, and a few brief notes, some of them upon the Fathers mentioned by him and his friends. For some of the latter I have to thank the Revd. V. Theokritov, Priest of the Russian Church in London.

R. M. F.

1

THE STARETS. *A year had gone by since I last saw the Pilgrim, when at length a gentle knock on the door and a pleading voice announced the arrival of that devout brother to the hearty welcome which awaited him.*

" Come in, dear brother ; let us thank God together for blessing your journey and bringing you back."

The Pilgrim. Praise and thanks be to the Father on high for His bounty in all things, which He orders as seems good to Him, and always for the good of us pilgrims and strangers in a strange land. Here am I, a sinner, who left you last year, again by the mercy of God thought worthy to see and hear your joyful welcome. And of course you are waiting to hear from me a full account of the Holy City of God, Jerusalem, for which my soul was longing and towards which my purpose was firmly set. But what we wish is not always carried out ; and so it was in my case. And no wonder, for why should I, a wretched sinner, be thought fit to tread that holy ground on which the divine footsteps of our Lord Jesus Christ were printed ?

You remember, Father, that I left here last year with a deaf old man as a companion, and that I had a letter from a merchant of Irkutsk to his son at Odessa asking him to send me to Jerusalem. Well, we got to Odessa all right in no very long time. My companion at once booked a passage on a ship for Constantinople and set off.

1

I for my part set about finding the merchant's son, by the address on the letter. I soon found his house, but there, to my surprise and sorrow, I learned that my benefactor was no longer alive. He had been dead and buried three weeks before, after a short illness. This made me very much cast down. But still, I trusted in the power of God. The whole household were in mourning, and the widow, who was left with three small children, was in such distress, that she wept all the time, and several times a day would collapse in grief. Her sorrow was so great that it seemed as though she too would not live long. All the same, in the midst of all this, she met me kindly, though in such a state of affairs she could not send me to Jerusalem. But she asked me to stay with her for a fortnight or so until her father-in-law came to Odessa, as he had promised, to settle the affairs of the bereaved family.

So I stayed. A week passed, a month, then another. But instead of coming the merchant wrote to say that his own affairs would not allow him to come, and advising that she should pay off the assistants, and that all should go to him at Irkutsk at once. So a great bustle and fuss began, and as I saw they were no longer interested in me, I thanked them for their hospitality and said good-bye. Once more I set off wandering about Russia.

I thought and thought. Where was I to go now? In the end I decided that first of all I would go to Kiev, where I had not been for many years. So I set off. Of course I fretted at first because I had not been able to carry out my wish to go to Jerusalem, but I reflected that even this had not happened without the providence of

God, and I quieted myself with the hope that God, the lover of men, would take the will for the deed, and would not let my wretched journey be without edification and spiritual value. And so it turned out, for I came across the sort of people who showed me many things that I did not know, and for my salvation brought light to my dark soul. If that necessity had not sent me on this journey I should not have met those spiritual benefactors of mine.

So by day I walked along with the Prayer, and in the evening when I halted for the night I read my *Philokalia*, for the strengthening and stimulating of my soul in its struggle with the unseen enemies of salvation.

On the road about forty-five miles from Odessa I met with an astonishing thing. There was a long train of wagons loaded with goods; there were about thirty of them, and I overtook them. The foremost driver, being the leader, was walking beside his horse, and the others were walking in a group some way from him. The road led past a pond which had a stream running through it, and in which the broken ice of the spring season was whirling about and piling up on the edges with a horrible noise. All of a sudden, the leading driver, a young man, stopped his horse, and the whole line of carts behind had to come to a standstill too. The other drivers came running up to him, and saw that he had begun to undress. They asked him why he was undressing. He answered that he very much wanted to bathe in the pond. Some of the astonished drivers began to laugh at him, others to scold him, calling him mad, and the eldest there, his own brother, tried to stop him, giving him a push to make him

3

drive on. The other defended himself and had not the least wish to do as he was told. Several of the young drivers started getting water out of the pond in the buckets with which they watered the horses, and for a joke splashed it over the man who wanted to bathe, on his head, or from behind, saying, "There you are; we'll give you a bath." As soon as the water touched his body, he cried out, "Ah, that's good," and sat down on the ground. They went on throwing water over him. Thereupon he soon lay down, and then and there quietly died. They were all in a great fright, having no idea why it had happened. The older ones bustled about, saying that the authorities ought to be told, while the rest came to the conclusion that it was his fate to meet this kind of death.

I stayed with them about an hour and then went on my way. About three and a half miles farther on I saw a village on the high road, and as I came into it I met an old priest walking along the street. I thought I would tell him about what I had just seen, and find out what he thought about it. The priest took me into his house, and I told him the story and asked him to explain to me the cause of what had taken place.

"I can tell you nothing about it, dear brother, except perhaps this, that there are many wonderful things in nature which our minds cannot understand. This, I think, is so ordered by God in order to show men the rule and providence of God in nature more clearly, through certain cases of unnatural and direct changes in its laws. It happens that I myself was once a witness of a similar case. Near our village there is a very deep and steep-sided ravine, not very wide, but some seventy feet or more in depth. It is quite frightening to look down to the gloomy bottom of it. A sort of footbridge has been built over it. A peasant in my parish, a family man and very respectable, suddenly, for no reason, was taken with an irresistible desire to throw himself from this little bridge into that deep ravine. He fought against the idea and resisted the impulse for a whole week. In the end, he could hold himself back no longer. He got up early, rushed off and jumped into the abyss. They soon heard his groans, and with great difficulty pulled him out of the pit with his legs broken. When he was asked the reason for his fall, he answered that although he was now feeling a great deal of pain, yet he was calm in spirit, that he had carried out the irresistible desire which had worried him so for a whole week, and that he had been ready to risk his life to gratify his wish.

"He was a whole year in hospital getting better. I used to go to see him, and often saw the doctors who were round him. Like you, I wanted to hear from them the cause of the affair. With one voice the doctors answered that it was 'frenzy.' When I asked them for a scientific explanation of what that was, and what caused it to attack a man, I could get nothing more out of them, except that this was one of the secrets of nature which were not revealed to science. I for my part observed that if in such a mystery of nature a man were to turn to God in prayer, and also to tell good people about it, then this un-governable 'frenzy' of theirs would not attain its purpose.

"Truly there is much to be met with in human life of which we can have no clear understanding."

While we were talking it was getting dark, and I stayed the night there. In the morning the mayor sent his secretary to ask the priest to bury the dead man in the cemetery, and to say that the doctors, after a *post-mortem*, had found no signs whatever of madness, and gave a sudden stroke as the cause of death.

"Look at that now," said the priest to me, "medical science can give no precise reason for his uncontrollable urge towards the water."

And so I said good-bye to the priest and went on my way. After I had travelled for several days and was feeling rather done-up, I came to a good-sized commercial town called Byelaya Tserkov. As evening was already coming on, I started to look around for a lodging for the night. In the market I came across a man who looked as though he was a traveller too. He was making enquiries among the shops for the address of a certain person who lived in the place. When he saw me he came up to me and said : "You look as though you are a pilgrim too, so let's go together and find a man by the name of Evreinov[1] who lives in this town. He is a good Christian and keeps a splendid inn, and he welcomes pilgrims. Look, I've got something written down about him." I gladly agreed, and so we soon found his house. Although the host himself was not at home, his wife, a nice old woman, received us very kindly and gave us an out-of-the-way private little garret in the attic to rest in. We settled down and rested for a while.

6

Then our host came, and asked us to have supper with them. During supper we talked—who we were and where we came from—and somehow or other the talk came round to the question of why he was called Evreinov. " I'll tell you an odd thing about that," he said, and began his story.

" You see, it was like this. My father was a Jew. He was born at Shklov, and he hated Christians. From his very earliest years he was preparing to be a rabbi and studied hard at all the Jewish chit-chat which was meant to disprove Christianity. One day he happened to be going through a Christian cemetery. He saw a human skull, which must have been taken out of some grave that had been recently disturbed. It had both its jaws and there were some horrible-looking teeth in them. In a fit of temper he began to jeer at this skull ; he spat at it, abused it and spurned it with his foot. Not content with that, he picked it up and stuck it on a post—as they stick up the bones of animals to drive off greedy birds. After amusing himself in this way, he went home. The following night he had scarcely fallen asleep when suddenly an unknown man appeared to him and violently upbraided him, saying, ' How dare you insult what is left of my poor bones ? I am a Christian—but as for you, you are the enemy of Christ.' The vision was repeated several times every night, and he got neither sleep nor rest. Then the same sight started flashing before his eyes during the daytime also, and he would hear the echo of that reproachful voice. As time went on the vision got more frequent, and in the end he began to feel depressed and frightened and to lose strength. He went to his rabbi, who read prayers and exorcisms over him. But the apparition not only did not cease; it got even more frequent and threatening.

" This state of affairs became known, and, hearing about it, a business friend of his, a Christian, began to advise him to accept the Christian religion, and to urge upon him that apart from that there was no way of ridding himself of this disturbing apparition of his. But the Jew was loth to take this step. However, in reply he said : ' I would gladly do as you wish, if only I could be free from this tormenting and intolerable apparition.' The Christian was glad to hear this, and persuaded him to send in to the local Bishop a request for baptism and reception into the Christian Church. The request was written and the Jew, not very eagerly, signed it. And lo and behold, the very minute that the request was signed, the apparition came to an end and never troubled him again. His joy was unbounded, and entirely at rest in mind he felt such a burning faith in Jesus Christ that he went straight away to the Bishop, told him the whole story, and expressed a heartfelt desire to be christened. He eagerly and quickly learned the dogmas of the Christian faith, and after his baptism he came to live in this town. Here he married my mother, a good Christian woman. He led a devout and very comfortable life and he was most generous to the poor. He taught me to be the same, and before his death gave me his instructions about this, together with his blessing. There you are ; that's why my name is Evreinov." [1]

I listened to this story with reverence and humility, and I thought to myself: "How good and kind our Lord Jesus Christ is, and how great is His love! In what different ways He draws sinners to Himself. With what wisdom He uses things of little importance to lead on to great things. Who could have expected that the mischievous pranks of a Jew with some dead bones would bring him to the true knowledge of Jesus Christ and be the means of leading him to a devout life?"

After supper we thanked God and our host, and retired to our garret. We did not want to go to bed yet, so we went on talking to each other. My companion told me that he was a merchant of Mogilev, and that he had spent two years in Bessarabia as a novice in one of the monasteries there, but only with a passport that expired at a fixed date. He was now on his way home to get the consent of the merchant community to his finally entering upon the monastic life. "The monasteries there satisfy me, their constitution and order, and the strict life of many devout *startsi* who live there." He assured me that putting the Bessarabian monasteries beside the Russian was like comparing heaven with earth. He urged me to do the same.

While we were talking about these things they brought still a third lodger into our room. This was a non-commissioned officer with the army for the time being, but now going home on leave. We saw that he was tired out with his journey. We said our prayers together and lay down to sleep. We were up early next morning and began to get ready for the road, and we only just wanted to go and thank our host, when suddenly we heard the bells ringing for Mattins. The merchant and I began to consider what we would do. How could we start after hearing the bells and without going to church? It would be better to stay to Mattins, say our prayers in church, and then we should go off more happily. So we decided: and we called the officer. But he said: "What's the point of going to church while you are on a journey? What good is it to God if we have been? Let's get off home and then say our prayers. You two go if you want. I'm not going. By the time you have stood through Mattins I shall be three or four miles or so farther on my way, and I want to get home as quickly as possible." To this the merchant said: "Look here, brother, don't you run so far ahead with your schemes until you know what God's plans are!" So we went to church, and he took the road.

We stayed through Mattins and the Liturgy too. Then we went back to our garret to get our knapsacks ready for the start, when what do we see but our hostess bringing in the *samovar*. "Where are you off to?" she says. "You must have a cup of tea—yes, and have dinner with us too. We can't send you away hungry." So we stayed. We had not been sitting at the *samovar* for half an hour, when all of a sudden our non-commissioned officer comes running in, all out of breath.

"I've come to you in both sorrow and joy."

"What's all this?" we asked him.

This is what he said:

"When I left you and started off, I thought I would look in at the pub to get change for a note, and have a

drink at the same time so as to get along better. So I
did. I got my change, had my drink, and was off like a
bird. When I had gone about two miles I had a mind to
count the money the fellow at the pub had given me. I
sat down by the roadside, took out my pocket-book, and
went through it. All serene. Then suddenly it struck
me that my passport was not there. Only some papers
and the money. I was as frightened as if I'd lost my
head. I saw in a flash what had happened. Of course
I had dropped it when I was settling up at the pub. I
must run back. I ran and ran. Another awful idea
seized me : suppose it's not there ! that will mean
trouble ! I rushed up to the man behind the bar and
asked him. ' I've not seen it,' he said. And was I
downhearted ! Well, I searched around and hunted
everywhere, wherever I had stood and hung about. And
what do you think ? I was lucky enough to find my passport. There it was, still folded up and lying on the floor
among the straw and litter, all trampled in the dirt.
Thank God ! I was glad, I can tell you ; it was as though
a mountain had rolled off my shoulders. Of course it was
filthy and coated with mud, enough to get me a clout on
the head ; still, that doesn't matter. At any rate I can
get home and back again with a whole skin. But I came
to tell you about it. And what's more, in my fright I've
rubbed my foot absolutely raw with running and I can't
possibly walk. So I came to ask for some grease to
bandage it up with.''

"There you are, brother," the merchant began ;
" that's because you wouldn't listen and come with us to

church. You wanted to get a long way ahead of us, and, on the contrary, here you are back again, and lame into the bargain. I told you not to run so far ahead with your schemes; and now see how it has turned out. It was a small thing that you did not come to church, but beside that you used such language as, ' What good does it do God if we pray ? ' That, brother, was bad. Of course, God does not need our sinful prayers, but, still, in His love for us He likes us to pray. And it is not only that holy prayer which the Holy Spirit Himself helps us to offer and arouses in us that is pleasing to Him, for He asks that of us when He says *Abide in Me, and I in you*; but every intention, every impulse, even every thought which is directed to His glory and our own salvation, is of value in His sight. For all these the boundless loving kindness of God gives bountiful rewards. The love of God gives grace a thousandfold more than human actions deserve. If you give Him the merest mite, He will pay you back with gold. If you but purpose to go to the Father, He will come out to meet you. You say but a word, short and unfeeling—' Receive me, have mercy on me '—and He falls on your neck and kisses you. That is what the love of the Heavenly Father is like towards us, unworthy as we are. And simply because of this love He rejoices in every gesture we make towards salvation, however small. It looks like this to you : What glory is there for God, what advantage for you, if you pray a little and then your thoughts wander again, or if you do some small good deed, such as reading a prayer, making five or ten acts of reverence, or giving a heartfelt sigh and calling upon the Name of Jesus, or attending to some good thought, or setting yourself to some spiritual reading, or abstaining from some food, or bearing an affront in silence—all that seems to you not enough for your full salvation and a fruitless thing to do. No! none of these small acts is in vain; it will be taken into account by the all-seeing eye of God, and receive a hundredfold reward, not only in eternity, but in this life. St. John Chrysostom asserts this. 'No good of any sort,' he says, 'however trifling it may be, will be scorned by the righteous Judge. If sins are searched out in such detail that we shall give an answer for words and desires and thoughts, then so much the more good deeds, however small they are, will be taken into account in all detail, and will be reckoned to our merit before our Judge, who is full of love.'

"I will tell you a case which I saw myself last year. In the Bessarabian monastery where I lived there was a *starets*, a monk of good life. One day a temptation beset him. He felt a great longing for some dried fish. And as it was impossible to get any in the monastery at that time, he was planning to go to the market and buy some. For a long while he struggled against the idea, and reasoned with himself that a monk ought to be content with the ordinary food provided for the brothers and by all means to avoid self-indulgence. Moreover, to walk about the market among crowds of people was also for a monk a source of temptation, and unseemly. In the end the lies of the Enemy got the upper hand of his reasoning, and he, yielding to his self-will, made up his mind and went for the fish. After he had left the building and was going along the street, he noticed that his rosary was not in his hand, and he began to think : ' How comes this, that I am going like a soldier without his sword ? This is most unseemly. And lay-folk who meet me will criticize me and fall into temptation, seeing a monk without his rosary ! ' He was going back to get it, but, feeling in his pocket, he found it there. He pulled it out, crossed himself, and with his rosary in his hand went calmly on. As he got near the market he saw a horse standing by a shop with a great cart-load of enormous tubs. All at once this horse, taking fright at something or other, bolted with all its might and with thundering hoofs made straight for him, grazing his shoulder and throwing him to the ground, though not hurting him very much. Then, a couple of paces from him, that load toppled over and the cart was smashed to splinters. Getting up quickly, naturally he was frightened enough, but at the same time he marvelled how God had saved his life, for if the load had fallen a split second earlier, then he would have been smashed to pieces like the cart. Thinking no further about it, he bought the fish, went back, ate it, said his prayers, and lay down to sleep.

" He slept lightly, and in his sleep a benign-looking *starets* whom he did not know appeared to him, and said : ' Listen, I am the protector of this dwelling, and I wish to teach you so that you will understand and remember the lesson now given you. Look now : the feeble effort you made against the feeling of pleasure, and your sloth in self-understanding and self-control, gave the Enemy his chance to attack you. He had got ready for you that fatal bombshell which exploded before your eyes. But your guardian angel foresaw this and put into your mind the thought of offering a prayer and remembering your rosary. Since you listened to this suggestion, obeyed and put it into action, it was just this that saved you from death. Do you see God's love for men, and His bountiful reward of even a slight turning towards Him?' Saying this, the visionary *starets* quickly left the cell. The monk bowed down at his feet, and in doing so woke up, to find himself, not on his bed, but kneeling prostrate at the threshold of the door. He told the story of this vision for the spiritual benefit of many people, myself among them.

"Truly boundless is the love of God for us sinners. Is it not marvellous that so small an action—yes, just taking his rosary out of his pocket and carrying it in his hand and calling once upon the Name of God—that that should give a man his life, and that in the scales of judgment upon men one short moment of calling upon Jesus Christ should outweigh many hours of sloth? In truth, here is the repayment of the tiny mite with gold. Do you see, brother, how powerful prayer is and how mighty the Name of Jesus when we call upon it? St. John Karpathisky in *The Philokalia* says that when in the Prayer of Jesus we call upon the Holy Name and say, 'Have mercy on me, a sinner,' then to every such petition the Voice of God answers in secret, 'Son, thy sins be forgiven thee.' And he goes on to say that when we say the Prayer there is at that moment nothing to distinguish us from the saints, confessors and martyrs. For, as St.

Chrysostom says, ' Prayer, although we are full of sin when we utter it, immediately cleanses us. God's loving-kindness to us is great, yet we sinners are listless, are not willing to give even one small hour to God in thanksgiving, and barter the time of prayer, which is more important than anything, for the bustle and cares of living, forgetting God and our duty. For that reason we often meet with misfortunes and calamities, yet even these the all-loving providence of God uses for our instruction and to turn our hearts to Him.' "

When the merchant came to the end of his talk to the officer, I said to him : " What comfort you have brought to my sinful soul too, your honour ! I could bow down to your very feet." Hearing this, he began to speak to me. " Ah, it seems you are a lover of religious stories. Wait a moment and I'll read you another like the one I have just told him. I've got here a book I travel with called *Agapia* ; or, *The Salvation of Sinners*. There are a lot of wonderful things in it."

He took the book out of his pocket and started reading a most beautiful story about one Agathonik, a devout man who from his childhood had been taught by pious parents to say every single day before the icon of the Mother of God the prayer which begins " Rejoice, God-bearing Maiden." And this he always did. Later, when he had grown up and started life on his own, he got absorbed in the cares and fuss of life and said the prayer but rarely, and finally gave it up altogether.

One day he gave a pilgrim a lodging for the night, who told him he was a hermit from the Thebaid and that he had seen a vision in which he was told to go to Agathonik and rebuke him for having given up the prayer to the Mother of God. Agathonik said the reason was that he had said the prayer for many years without seeing any result whatever. Then the hermit said to him: "Remember, blind and thankless one, how many times this prayer has helped you and saved you from disaster. Remember how in your youth you were wonderfully saved from drowning. Do you not recall that an epidemic of infectious disease carried off many of your friends to the grave, but you remained in health? Do you remember, when you were driving with a friend, you both fell out of the cart; he broke his leg, but you were unhurt? Do you not know that a young man of your acquaintance who used to be well and strong is now lying weak and ill, whereas you are in good health and feel no pain?" And he reminded Agathonik of many other things. In the end he said: "Know this, that all those troubles were warded off from you by the protection of the most holy Mother of God because of that short prayer, by which you lifted up your heart every day into union with God. Take care now, go on with it, and do not give up praising the Queen of Heaven lest she should forsake you."

When he had finished reading they called us to dinner, and afterwards, feeling our strength renewed, we thanked our host and took the road. We parted, and each went his own way as seemed best to him.

After that I walked on for about five days, cheered by the memory of the stories I had heard from the good

merchant in Byelaya Tserkov, and I began to get near to
Kiev. All at once and for no reason at all I began to feel
dull and heavy and my thoughts got gloomy and dispirited.
The Prayer went with difficulty and a sort of indolence
came over me. So, seeing a wood with a thick under-
growth of bushes by the side of the road, I went into it to
rest a bit, looking for some out-of-the-way place where
I could sit under a bush and read my *Philokalia*, and so
arouse my feeble spirit and comfort my faintheartedness.
I found a quiet place and began to read Kassian the Roman
in the fourth part of *The Philokalia*—on the Eight
Thoughts. When I had been reading happily for about
half an hour, quite unexpectedly I noticed the figure of a
man some hundred yards or so away from me and farther
in the forest. He was kneeling quite motionless. I was
glad to see this, for I gathered, of course, that he was
praying, and I began to read again. I went on reading for
an hour or more and then glanced up again. The man
was still kneeling there and never stirred. All this moved
me very much and I thought, What devout servants of
God there are!

As I was turning it over in my mind, the man suddenly
fell to the ground and lay still. This startled me, and as
I had not seen his face, for he had been kneeling with his
back to me, I felt curious to go and see who he was.
When I got to him I found him in a light sleep. He was
a country lad, a young fellow of about twenty-five. He
had an attractive face, good-looking, but pale. He was
dressed in a peasant's caftan with a bast rope for a girdle.
There was nothing else to note about him. He had no

kotomka,[2] not even a stick. The sound of my approach awoke him and he got up. I asked him who he was, and he told me he was a State peasant of the Smolensk Government and that he was on his way from Kiev.

" And where are you going to now ? " I asked.

" I don't know myself where God will lead me," he answered.

" Is it long since you left home ? "

" Yes, over four years."

" And where have you been living all that time ? "

" I have been going from shrine to shrine and to monasteries and churches. There was no point in staying at home. I'm an orphan and I have no relations. Besides, I've got a lame foot. So I'm roaming about the wide world."

" Some God-fearing person, it seems, has taught you not just to roam anywhere, but to visit holy places," said I.

" Well, you see," he answered, " having no father or mother, I used to go about as a boy with the shepherds of our village, and all went happily enough till I was ten years old. Then one day when I had brought the flock home I never noticed that the *starosta's*[3] very best sheep was not among them. And our *starosta* was a bad and inhuman peasant. When he came home that evening and found that his sheep was lost, he rushed at me abusing and threatening. If I didn't go off and find the sheep, he swore he'd beat me to death, and ' I'll break your arms and legs,' he said. Knowing how cruel he was, I went after the sheep, searching the places where they had been feeding in daylight. I searched and searched for more

than half the night, but there was not a trace of it anywhere. It was such a dark night, too, for it was getting on
towards autumn. When I had got very deep into the
forest—and in our government the forests are endless—
suddenly a storm got up. It was as though the trees
were all rocking. In the distance wolves started howling.
Such a terror fell upon me that my hair stood on end.
What's more, it all got more and more horrible, so that
I was ready to drop with fear and horror. Then I fell on
my knees and crossed myself, and with all my heart I said :
' Lord Jesus Christ, have mercy on me.' As soon as I had
said that I felt absolutely at peace, straight away, as if
I had never been in any distress at all. All my fear left
me and I felt as happy in my heart as if I had flown away
to heaven. This made me very glad, and—well, I just
didn't stop saying the Prayer. To this day I don't know
whether the storm lasted long and how the night went.
I looked up and daylight was coming, and there was I still
kneeling in the same place. I got up quietly, I saw I
shouldn't find the sheep, and home I went. But all was
well in my heart and I was saying the Prayer to my heart's
content. As soon as I got to the village the *starosta* saw I
hadn't brought the sheep back and thrashed me till I was
half dead—he put this foot out of joint, you see. I was
laid up, almost unable to move, for six weeks after that
beating. All I knew was that I was saying the Prayer
and it comforted me. When I got a bit better I began to
wander about in the world, and as to be continually
jostling about in a crowd didn't interest me, and meant
a good deal of sin, I took to roaming from one holy place

to another, and in the forests too. That's how I have spent nearly five years now."

When I heard this, my heart was very glad that God had thought me fit to meet so good a man, and I asked him, "And do you often use the Prayer now?"

"I couldn't exist without it," he answered. "Why, if I only just call to mind how I felt that first time in the forest, it's just as if someone pushed me down on my knees and I begin to pray. I don't know whether my sinful prayer is pleasing to God or not. For as I pray, sometimes I feel a great happiness—why, I don't know—a lightness of spirit, a happy sort of quiet; but at other times I feel a dull heaviness and lowness of spirits. But for all that, I want to go on praying always till I die."

"Don't be distressed, dear brother. Everything is pleasing to God and for our salvation—everything, whatever it is that happens in time of prayer. So the holy Fathers say. Whether it's lightness of heart or heaviness, it's all all right. No prayer, good or bad, fails in God's sight. Lightness, warmth and gladness show that God is rewarding and consoling us for the effort, while heaviness, darkness and dryness mean that God is cleansing and strengthening the soul, and by this wholesome trial is saving it, preparing it in humility for the enjoyment of blessed happiness in the future. In proof of this I will read you something that St. John Klimax wrote."

I found the passage and read it to him. He heard it through with care and enjoyed it, and he thanked me very much for it. And so we parted. He went off right into the depth of the forest and I went back to the road. I went on my way, thanking God for treating me, sinner as I am, as fit to be given such teaching.

Next day, by God's help, I came to Kiev. The first and chief thing I wanted was to fast a while and to make my Confession and Communion in that holy town. So I stopped near the saints,[4] as that would be easier for getting to church. A good old Cossack took me in, and as he lived alone in his hut, I found peace and quiet there. At the end of a week, in which I had been getting ready for my Confession, the thought came to me that I would make it as detailed as I could. So I began to recall and go over all my sins from youth onwards very fully, and so as not to forget it all I wrote down everything I could remember in the utmost detail. I covered a large sheet of paper with it.

I heard that at Kitaevaya Pustina, about five miles from Kiev, there was a priest of ascetic life who was very wise and understanding. Whoever went to him for Confession found an atmosphere of tender compassion, and came away with teaching for his salvation and ease of spirit. I was very glad to hear of this and I went to him at once. After I had asked his advice and we had talked awhile, I gave him my sheet of paper to see. He read it through, and then said : " Dear friend, a lot of this that you have written is quite futile. Listen : first, don't bring into Confession sins which you have already repented of and had forgiven. Don't go over them again, for that would be to doubt the power of the sacrament of penance. Next : don't call to mind other people who have been connected with your sins ; judge yourself only.

Thirdly : the holy Fathers forbid us to mention all the circumstances of the sins, and tell us to acknowledge them in general, so as to avoid temptation both for ourselves and for the priest. Fourthly : you have come to repent and you are not repenting of the fact that you can't repent—*i.e.*, you penitence is lukewarm and careless. Fifthly : you have gone over all these details, but the most important thing you have overlooked : you have not disclosed the gravest sins of all. You have not acknowledged, nor written down, that you do not love God, that you hate your neighbour, that you do not believe in God's Word, and that you are filled with pride and ambition. A whole mass of evil, and all our spiritual depravity is in these four sins. They are the chief roots out of which spring the shoots of all the sins into which we fall.''

I was very much surprised to hear this, and I said : '' Forgive me, reverend Father, but how is it possible not to love God our Creator and Preserver ? What is there to believe in if not the Word of God, in which everything is true and holy ? I wish well to all my neighbours, and why should I hate them ? I have nothing to be proud of ; besides having numberless sins, I have nothing at all which is fit to be praised, and what should I with my poverty and ill-health lust after ? Of course, if I were an educated man, or rich, then no doubt I should be guilty of the things you spoke of.''

'' It's a pity, dear one, that you so little understood what I said. Look ! It will teach you more quickly if I give you these notes. They are what I always use for my

23

own Confession. Read them through, and you will see clearly enough an exact proof of what I said to you just now."

He gave me the notes, and I began to read them, as follows:

"A Confession which Leads the Inward Man to Humility.

"Turning my eyes carefully upon myself and watching the course of my inward state, I have verified by experience that I do not love God, that I have no love for my neighbours, that I have no religious belief, and that I am filled with pride and sensuality. All this I actually find in myself as a result of detailed examination of my feelings and conduct, thus:

"1. *I do not love God.* For if I loved God I should be continually thinking about Him with heartfelt joy. Every thought of God would give me gladness and delight. On the contrary, I much more often and much more eagerly think about earthly things, and thinking about God is labour and dryness. If I loved God, then talking with Him in prayer would be my nourishment and delight and would draw me to unbroken communion with Him. But, on the contrary, I not only find no delight in prayer, but even find it an effort. I struggle with reluctance, I am enfeebled by sloth, and am ready to occupy myself eagerly with any unimportant trifle, if only it shortens prayer and keeps me from it. My time slips away unnoticed in futile occupations, but when I am occupied with God, when I put myself into His presence every hour seems like a year. If one person loves another, he thinks of him throughout the day without ceasing, he pictures him to himself, he cares for him, and in all circumstances his beloved friend is never out of his thoughts. But I, throughout the day, scarcely set aside even a single hour in which to sink deep down into meditation upon God, to inflame my heart with love of Him, while I eagerly give up twenty-three hours as fervent offerings to the idols of my passions. I am forward in talk about frivolous matters and things which degrade the spirit; that gives me pleasure. But in the consideration of God I am dry, bored and lazy. Even if I am unwillingly drawn by others into spiritual conversation, I try to shift the subject quickly to one which pleases my desires. I am tirelessly curious about novelties, about civic affairs and political events; I eagerly seek the satisfaction of my love of knowledge in science and art, and in ways of getting things I want to possess. But the study of the Law of God, the knowledge of God and of religion, make little impression on me, and satisfy no hunger of my soul. I regard these things not only as a non-essential occupation for a Christian, but in a casual way as a sort of side-issue with which I should perhaps occupy my spare time, at odd moments. To put it shortly, if love for God is recognized by the keeping of His commandments (*If ye love Me, keep My commandments*, says our Lord Jesus Christ), and I not only do not keep them, but even make little attempt to do so, then in absolute truth the conclusion follows that I do not love God. That is what Basil the Great says: ' The proof that a man does not love God and His Christ lies in the fact that he does not keep His commandments.'

" 2. *I do not love my neighbour either.* For not only am I unable to make·up my mind to lay down my life for his sake (according to the Gospel), but I do not even sacrifice my happiness, well-being and peace for the good of my neighbour. If I did love him as myself, as the Gospel bids, his misfortunes would distress me also, his happiness would bring delight to me too. But, on the contrary, I listen to curious, unhappy stories about my neighbour, and I am not distressed ; I remain quite undisturbed or, what is still worse, I find a sort of pleasure in them. Bad conduct on the part of my brother I do not cover up with love, but proclaim abroad with censure. His well-being, honour and happiness do not delight me as my own, and, as if they were something quite alien to me, give me no feeling of gladness. What is more, they subtly arouse in me feelings of envy or contempt.

" 3. *I have no religious belief.* Neither in immortality nor in the Gospel. If I were firmly persuaded and believed without doubt that beyond the grave lies eternal life and recompense for the deeds of this life, I should be continually thinking of this. The very idea of immortality would terrify me and I should lead this life as a foreigner who gets ready to enter his native land. On the contrary, I do not even think about eternity, and I regard the end of this earthly life as the limit of my existence. The secret thought nestles within me : Who knows what happens at death? If I say I believe in immortality, then I am speaking about my mind only, and my heart is far removed from a firm conviction about it. That is openly witnessed to by my conduct and my constant care to satisfy the life of the senses. Were the Holy Gospel taken into my heart in faith, as the Word of God, I should be continually occupied with it, I should study it, find delight in it and with deep devotion fix my attention upon it. Wisdom, mercy, love, are hidden in it; it would lead me to happiness, I should find gladness in the study of the Law of God day and night. In it I should find nourishment like my daily bread and my heart would be drawn to the keeping of its laws. Nothing on earth would be strong enough to turn me away from it. On the contrary, if now and again I read or hear the Word of God, yet even so it is only from necessity or from a general love of knowledge, and approaching it without any very close attention, I find it dull and uninteresting. I usually come to the end of the reading without any profit, only too ready to change over to secular reading in which I take more pleasure and find new and interesting subjects.

"4. *I am full of pride and sensual self-love.* All my actions confirm this. Seeing something good in myself, I want to bring it into view, or to pride myself upon it before other people or inwardly to admire myself for it. Although I display an outward humility, yet I ascribe it all to my own strength and regard myself as superior to others, or at least no worse than they. If I notice a fault in myself, I try to excuse it, I cover it up by saying, ' I am made like that ' or ' I am not to blame.' I get angry with those who do not treat me with respect and consider them unable to appreciate the value of people. I brag about my gifts: my failures in any undertaking I regard as a personal insult. I murmur, and I find pleasure in the unhappiness of my enemies. If I strive after anything good it is for the purpose of winning praise, or spiritual self-indulgence, or earthly consolation. In a word, I continually make an idol of myself and render it uninterrupted service, seeking in all things the pleasures of the senses, and nourishment for my sensual passions and lusts.

" Going over all this I see myself as proud, adulterous, unbelieving, without love to God and hating my neighbour. What state could be more sinful? The condition of the spirits of darkness is better than mine. They, although they do not love God, hate men, and live upon pride, yet at least believe and tremble. But I? Can there be a doom more terrible than that which faces me, and what sentence of punishment will be more severe than that upon the careless and foolish life that I recognize in myself?"

On reading through this form of Confession which the priest gave me I was horrified and I thought to myself: " Good Heavens! What frightful sins there are hidden within me and up to now I've never noticed them!" The desire to be cleansed from them made me beg this great spiritual father to teach me how to know the causes of all these evils and how to cure them. And he began to instruct me.

" You see, dear brother, the cause of not loving God is want of belief, want of belief is caused by lack of

28

conviction, and the cause of that is failure to seek for holy and true knowledge, indifference to the light of the spirit. In a word, if you don't believe, you can't love; if you are not convinced, you can't believe, and in order to reach conviction you must get a full and exact knowledge of the matter before you. By meditation, by the study of God's Word and by noting your experience, you must arouse in your soul a thirst and a longing—or, as some call it, ' wonder '—which brings you an insatiable desire to know things more closely and more fully, to go deeper into their nature.

" One spiritual writer speaks of it in this way : ' Love,' he says, ' usually grows with knowledge, and the greater the depth and extent of the knowledge the more love there will be, the more easily the heart will soften and lay itself open to the love of God, as it diligently gazes upon the very fullness and beauty of the divine nature and His unbounded love for men.'

" So now you see that the cause of those sins which you read over is slothfulness in thinking about spiritual things, sloth which stifles the feeling of the need of such thought. If you want to know how to overcome this evil, strive after enlightenment of spirit by every means in your power, attain it by diligent study of the Word of God and of the holy Fathers, by the help of meditation and spiritual counsel and by the conversation of those who are wise in Christ. Ah, dear brother, how much disaster we meet with just because we are lazy about seeking light for our souls through the word of truth. We do not study God's law day and night, and we do not pray about it diligently and unceasingly. And because of this our inner man is hungry and cold, starved, so that it has no strength to take a bold step forward upon the road of righteousness and salvation! And so, beloved, let us resolve to make use of these methods, and as often as possible fill our minds with thoughts of heavenly things; and love, poured down into our hearts from on high, will burst into flame within us. We will do this together and pray as often as we can, for prayer is the chief and strongest means for our renewal and well-being. We will pray, in the words Holy Church teaches us: ' O God, make me fit to love Thee now, as I have loved sin in the past.' "[5]

I listened to all this with care. Deeply moved, I asked this holy father to hear my Confession and to give me Communion. And so next morning after the honour of my Communion, I was for going back to Kiev with this blessed viaticum. But this good father of mine, who was going to the *Lavra*[6] for a couple of days, kept me for that time in his hermit's cell, so that in its silence I might give myself up to prayer without hindrance. And, in fact, I did spend both those days as though I was in heaven. By the prayers of my *starets* I, unworthy as I am, rejoiced in perfect peace. Prayer flowed out in my heart so easily and happily that during that time I think I forgot everything, and myself; in my mind was Jesus Christ and He alone.

In the end, the priest came back, and I asked his guidance and advice—where should I go now on my pilgrim way? He gave me his blessing with these words,

30

"You go to Pochaev, make your reverence there to the wonder-working Footprint[7] of the most pure Mother of God, and she will guide your feet into the way of peace." And so, taking his advice in faith, three days later I set off for Pochaev.

For some hundred and thirty miles or so I travelled none too happily, for the road lay through pot-houses and Jewish villages and I seldom came across a Christian dwelling. At one farm I noticed a Russian Christian inn and I was glad to see it. I turned in at it to spend the night and also to ask for some bread for my journey, for my rusks were coming to an end. Here I saw the host, an old man with a well-to-do air and who, I learned, came from the same government that I did—the Orlovsky. Directly I went into the room, his first question was : " What religion are you? "

I replied that I was a Christian, and *pravoslavny*.[8] " *Pravoslavny*, indeed," said he with a laugh. " You people are *pravoslavny* only in word—in act you are heathen. I know all about your religion, brother. A learned priest once tempted me and I tried it. I joined your Church, and stayed in it for six months. After that I came back to the ways of our society. To join your Church is just a snare. The readers mumble the service all anyhow, with things missed out and things you can't understand. And the singing is no better than you hear in a pub. And the people stand all in a huddle, men and women all mixed up ; they talk while the service is going on, turn round and stare about, walk to and fro and give you no peace and quiet to say your prayers. What sort of worship do you call that? It's just a sin! Now, with us how devout the service is; you can hear what's said, nothing is missed out, the singing is most moving and the people stand quietly, the men by themselves, the women by themselves, and everybody knows what reverence to make and when, as Holy Church directs. Really and truly, when you come into a church of ours, you feel you have come to the worship of God; but in one of yours you can't imagine what you've come to—to Church or to market!"

From all this I saw that the old man was a diehard *raskolnik*.[9] But he spoke so plausibly, I could not argue with him nor convert him. I just thought to myself that it will be impossible to convert the Old Believers to the true Church until church services are put right among us and until the clergy in particular set an example in this. The *raskolnik* knows nothing of the inner life; he relies upon externals, and it is about them that we are careless.

So I wanted to get away from here and had already gone out into the hall when to my surprise I saw through the open door of a private room a man who did not look like a Russian; he was lying on a bed and reading a book. He beckoned me and asked me who I was. I told him. And then he began: "Listen, dear friend. Won't you agree to look after a sick man, say for a week, until by God's help I get better? I am a Greek, a monk from Mount Athos. I'm in Russia to collect alms for my monastery and on my way back I've fallen ill, so that I can't walk for the pain in my legs. So I've taken this room here. Don't say no, servant of God! I'll pay you."

" There is no need whatever to pay me. I will very gladly look after you as best I can in the name of God." So I stayed with him. I heard a great deal from him about the things which concern the salvation of our souls. He told me about Athos, the Holy Mountain, about the great *podvizhniki*[10] there, and about the many hermits and anchorites. He had with him a copy of *The Philokalia* in Greek, and a book by Isaac the Syrian. We read together and compared the Slavonic translation by Paisy Velichovsky with the Greek original. He declared that it would be impossible to translate from Greek more accurately and faithfully than *The Philokalia* had been turned into Slavonic by Paisy.

As I noticed that he was always in prayer and versed in the inward prayer of the heart, and as he spoke Russian perfectly, I questioned him on this matter. He readily told me a great deal about it and I listened with care. I even wrote down many things that he said. Thus, for example, he taught me about the excellence and greatness of the Jesus Prayer in this way. " Even the very form of the Jesus Prayer," he said, " shows what a great prayer it is. It is made up of two parts. In the first, *i.e.*, ' Lord Jesus Christ, Son of God,' it leads our thoughts to the life of Jesus Christ, or, as the holy Fathers put it, it is the whole Gospel in brief. In the second part, ' Have mercy on me, a sinner,' it faces us with the story of our own helplessness and sinfulness. And it is to be noted that the desire and petition of a poor, sinful, humble soul could not be put into words more wise, more clear cut, more exact than these—' have mercy on me.' No other form of words would be as satisfying and full as this. For instance, if one said, ' Forgive me, put away my sins, cleanse my transgressions, blot out my offences,' all that would express one petition only—asking to be set free from punishment, the fear of a faint-hearted and listless soul. But to say ' Have mercy on me ' means not only the desire for pardon arising from fear, but is the sincere cry of filial love, which puts its hope in the mercy of God and humbly acknowledges it is too weak to break its own will and to keep a watchful guard over itself. It is a cry for mercy—that is, for grace—which will show itself in the gift of strength from God, to enable us to resist temptation and overcome our sinful inclinations. It is like a penniless debtor asking his kindly creditor not only to forgive him the debt but also to pity his extreme poverty and to give him alms—that is what these profound words ' have mercy on me ' express. It is like saying : ' Gracious Lord, forgive me my sins and help me to put myself right ; arouse in my soul a strong impulse to follow Thy bidding. Bestow Thy grace in forgiving my actual sins and in turning my heedless mind, will and heart to Thee alone.' "

Upon this I wondered at the wisdom of his words and thanked him for teaching my sinful soul, and he went on teaching me other wonderful things.

" If you like," said he (and I took him to be something of a scholar, for he said he had studied at the Athens Academy), " I will go on and tell you about the tone in which the Jesus Prayer is said. I happen to have heard many God-fearing Christian people say the oral Jesus

Prayer as the Word of God bids them and according to the tradition of Holy Church. They use it so both in their private prayers and in church. If you listen carefully and as a friend to this quiet saying of the Prayer, you can notice for your spiritual profit that the tone of the praying voice varies with different people. Thus, some stress the very first word of the Prayer and say *Lord* Jesus Christ, and then finish all the other words on one level tone. Others begin the Prayer in a level voice and throw the stress in the middle of the Prayer, on the word *Jesus* as an exclamation, and the rest, again, they finish in an unstressed tone, as they began. Others, again, begin and go on with the Prayer without stress until they come to the last words—*Have mercy on me*—when they raise their voices in ecstasy. And some say the whole Prayer—Lord Jesus Christ, Son of God, have mercy on me a sinner—with all the stress upon the single phrase—*Son of God*.

"Now listen. The Prayer is one and the same. Orthodox Christians hold one and the same profession of faith. The knowledge is common to all of them, that this sublime Prayer of all prayers includes two things: the Lord Jesus and the appeal to Him. That is known to be the same for everybody. Why then do they not all express it in the same way, why not all in the same tone, that is? Why does the soul plead specially, and express itself with particular stress, not in one and the same place for all, but in a certain place for each? Many say of this that perhaps it is the result of habit, or of copying other people, or that it depends upon a way of understanding the words which corresponds with the individual point of view, or finally that it is just as it comes most easily and naturally to each person. But I think quite differently about it. I should like to look for something higher in it, something unknown not only to the listener, but even to the person who is praying also. May there not be here a hidden moving of the Holy Spirit *making intercession for us with groanings which cannot be uttered* in those who do not know how and about what to pray? And if everyone prays in the Name of Jesus Christ, by the Holy Spirit, as the Apostle says, the Holy Spirit, who works in secret and gives a prayer to him who prays, may also bestow His beneficent gift upon all, notwithstanding their lack of strength. To one He may give the reverent fear of God, to another love, to another firmness of faith, and to another gracious humility, and so on.

" If this be so, then he who has been given the gift of revering and praising the power of the Almighty will in his prayers stress with special feeling the word *Lord* in which he feels the greatness and the might of the Creator of the world. He who has been given the secret out-pouring of love in his heart is thrown into rapture and filled with gladness as he exclaims *Jesus Christ*, just as a certain *starets* could not hear the Name of Jesus without a peculiar flood of love and gladness, even in ordinary conversation. The unshakable believer in the Godhead of Jesus Christ, of one Substance with the Father, is enkindled with still more fervent faith as he says the words *Son of God*. One who has received the gift of humility and is deeply aware of his own weakness, with the words *have mercy on me* is penitent and humbled, and pours out his heart most richly in these last words of the Jesus Prayer. He cherishes hope in the loving kindness of God and abhors his own falling into sin. There you have the causes, in my opinion, of the differing tones in which people say the Prayer in the Name of Jesus. And from this you may note as you listen, to the glory of God and your own instruction, by what emotion any one is specially moved, what spiritual gift any one person has. A number of people have said to me on this subject : 'Why do not all these signs of hidden spiritual gifts appear together and united? Then not only one, but every word of the Prayer would be imbued with one and the same tone of rapture.' I have answered in this way : 'Since the grace of God distributes His gift in wisdom to every man severally according to his strength, as we see from Holy Scripture, who can search out with his finite mind and enter into the dispositions of grace? Is not the clay completely in the power of the potter, and is he not able to make one thing or another out of the clay?'"

I spent five days with this *starets*, and he began to get very much better in health. This time was of so much profit to me that I did not notice how quickly it went. For in that little room, in silent seclusion, we were concerned with nothing else whatever than silent prayer in the Name of Jesus, or talk about the same subject, interior prayer.

One day a pilgrim came to see us. He complained bitterly about the Jews and abused them. He had been going about their villages and had to put up with their unfriendliness and cheating. He was so bitter against them that he cursed them, even saying they were not fit to live because of their obstinacy and unbelief. Finally he said that he had such an aversion for them that it was quite beyond his control.

" You have no right, friend," said the *starets*, " to abuse and curse the Jews like this. God made them just as He made us. You should be sorry for them and pray for them not curse them. Believe me, the disgust you feel for them comes from the fact that you are not grounded in the love of God and have no interior prayer as a security and, therefore, no inward peace. I will read you a passage from the holy Fathers about this. Listen, this is what Mark the Podvizhnik writes : ' The soul which is inwardly united to God becomes, in the greatness of its joy, like a good-natured simple-hearted child, and now condemns no one, Greek, heathen, Jew nor sinner, but looks at them all alike with sight that has been cleansed, finds joy in the whole world, and wants everybody— Greeks and Jews and heathen—to praise God.' And Macarius the Great, of Egypt, says that the inward contemplative ' burns with so great a love that if it were possible he would have everyone to dwell within him, making no difference between bad and good.' There, dear brother, you see what the holy Fathers think about it. So I advise you to lay aside your fierceness, and look upon everything as under the all-knowing providence of God, and when you meet with vexations accuse yourself especially of lack of patience and humility.

At last more than a week went by and my *starets* got

well, and I thanked him from my heart for all the blessed instruction that he had given me, and we said good-bye. He set off for home and I started upon the way I had planned. Now I began to get near to Pochaev. I had not gone more than seventy miles when a soldier overtook me and I asked him where he was going. He told me he was going back to his native district in Kamenets Podolsk. We went along in silence for seven miles or so, and I noticed that he sighed very heavily as though something was distressing him, and he was very gloomy. I asked him why he was so sad.

"Good friend, if you have noticed my sorrow and will swear by all you hold sacred never to tell anybody, I will tell you all about myself, for I am near to death and I have no one to talk to about it."

I assured him, as a Christian, that I had not the slightest need to tell anybody about it, and that out of brotherly love I should be glad to give him any advice that I could.

"Well, you see," he began, "I was drafted as a soldier from the State Peasants. After about five years' service it became intolerably hard for me; in fact, they often flogged me for negligence and for drunkenness. I took it into my head to run away, and here I am a deserter for the last fifteen years. For six years I hid wherever I could. I stole from farms and larders and warehouses. I stole horses. I broke into shops and followed this sort of trade, always on my own. I got rid of my stolen goods in various ways. I drank the money, I led a depraved life, committed every sin. Only my soul didn't perish. I got on very well, but in the end I got into gaol for wandering without a passport. But when a chance came I even escaped from there. Then unexpectedly I met with a soldier who had been discharged from the service and was going home to a distant government; and as he was ill and could hardly walk he asked me to take him to the nearest village where he could find a lodging. So I took him. The police allowed us to spend the night in a barn on some hay and there we lay down. When I woke up in the morning I glanced at my soldier and there he was dead and stiff. Well, I hurriedly searched for his passport—that is to say, his discharge—and when I found it and a fair amount of money too, while everybody was still asleep, I was out of that shed and the back yard as quickly as I could, and so into the forest, and off I went. On reading his passport I saw that in age and distinguishing marks he was almost the same as I. I was very glad about this and went on boldly into the depths of the Astrakhan Government. There I began to steady down a bit and I got a job as a labourer. I joined up with an old man there who had his own house and was a cattle dealer. He lived alone with his daughter, who was a widow. When I had lived with him for a year I married this daughter of his. Then the old man died. We could not carry on the business. I started drinking again, and my wife too, and in a year we had got through everything the old man had left. And then my wife took ill and died. So I sold everything that was left, and the house, and I soon ran through the money.

" Now I had nothing to live on, nothing to eat. So I went back to my old trade of dealing in stolen goods, and all the more boldly now because I had a passport. So I took to my old evil life again for about a year. There came a time when for a long while I met with no success. I stole an old wretched horse from a *bobil* [11] and I sold it to the knackers for a bob. Taking the money, I went off to a pub and began to drink. I had an idea of going to a village where there was a wedding, and while everybody was asleep after the feasting I meant to pick up whatever I could. As the sun had not yet set I went into the forest to wait for night. I lay down there and fell into a deep sleep. Then I had a dream and saw myself standing in a wide and beautiful meadow. Suddenly a terrible cloud began to rise in the sky, and then there came such a terrific clap of thunder that the ground trembled underneath me and it was as though someone drove me up to my shoulders into the ground which jammed against me on all sides. Only my head and my hands were left outside. Then this terrible cloud seemed to come down on to the ground and out of it came my grandfather, who had been dead for twenty years. He was a very upright man and for thirty years was a churchwarden in our village. With an angry and threatening face he came up to me and I shook with fear. Round about nearby I saw several heaps of things which I had stolen at various times. I was still more frightened. My grandfather came up to me and, pointing to the first heap, said threateningly: ' What is that? Let him have it!' And suddenly the ground on all sides of me began to squeeze me so hard that I could not bear the pain and the faintness. I groaned and cried out, ' Have mercy on me,' but the torment went on. Then my grandfather pointed to another heap and said again: 'What is that? Crush him harder!' And I felt such violent pain and agony that no torture on earth could compare with it. Finally, that grandfather of mine brought near me the horse that I had stolen the evening before, and cried out: 'And what is this? Let him have it as hard as you can.' And I got such pain from all sides that I can't describe it; it was so cruel, terrible and exhausting. It was as though all my sinews were being drawn out of me and I was suffocated by the frightful pain. I felt I could not bear it and that I should collapse unconscious if that torture went on even a little bit longer. But the horse kicked out and caught me on the cheek and cut it open, and the moment I got that blow I woke up in utter horror and shaking like a weakling. I saw that it was already daylight, the sun was rising. I touched my cheek and blood was flowing from it; and those parts of me which in my dream had been in the ground were all, so to say, hard and stiff and I had pins and needles in them. I was in such terror that I could hardly get up and go home. My cheek hurt for a long time. Look, you can see the scar now. It wasn't there before. And so, after this, fear and horror often used to come over me and now I only have to remember what I suffered in that dream for the agony and exhaustion to begin again and such torture that I don't know what to do with myself. What is more, it began to come more often, and in the end I began to be afraid of people and to feel ashamed as though everybody knew my past dishonesty. Then I could neither eat nor

42

drink nor sleep because of this suffering. I was worn to a ravel. I did think of going to my regiment and making a clean breast of everything. Perhaps God would forgive my sins if I took my punishment. But I was afraid and I lost my courage because they would make me run the gauntlet. And so, losing patience, I wanted to hang myself. But the thought came to me that in any case I shan't live for a very long time; I shall soon die, for I have lost all my strength. And so I thought I would go and say good-bye to my home and die there. I have a nephew at home. And here I am on my way there for six months now. And all the while grief and fear make me miserable. What do you think, my friend? What am I to do? I really can't bear much more."

When I heard all this I was astonished and I praised the wisdom and the goodness of God, as I saw the different ways in which they are brought to sinners. So I said to him : " Dear brother, during the time of that fear and agony you ought to have prayed to God. That is the great cure for all our troubles."

" Not on your life ! " he said to me. " I thought that directly I began to pray God would destroy me."

" Nonsense, brother ; it is the Devil puts thoughts like that into your head. There is no end to God's mercy and He is sorry for sinners and quickly forgives all who repent. Perhaps you don't know the Jesus Prayer : ' Lord Jesus Christ, have mercy on me, a sinner.' You go on saying that without stopping."

" Why, of course I know that Prayer. I used to say

it sometimes to keep my courage up when I was going to do a robbery."

" Now, look here. God did not destroy you when you were on your way to do something wrong and said the Prayer. Will He do so when you start praying on the path of repentance? Now, you see how your thoughts come from the Devil. Believe me, dear brother, if you will say that Prayer, taking no notice of whatever thoughts come into your mind, then you will quickly feel relief. All the fear and strain will go and in the end you will be completely at peace. You will become a devout man and all sinful passions will leave you. I assure you of this, for I have seen a great deal of it in my time."

After that I told him about several cases in which the Jesus Prayer had shown its wonderful power to work upon sinners. In the end I persuaded him to come with me to the Pochaev Mother of God, the refuge of sinners, before he went home, and to make his Confession and Communion there.

My soldier listened to all this attentively and, as I could see, with joy, and he agreed to everything. We went to Pochaev together on this condition, that neither of us should speak to the other, but that we should say the Jesus Prayer all the time. In this silence we walked for a whole day. Next day he told me that he felt much easier and it was plain that his mind was calmer than before. On the third day we arrived at Pochaev and I urged him again not to break off the Prayer either day or night while he was awake, and assured him that the most Holy Name of Jesus, which is unbearable to our spiritual foes, would be strong to save him. On this point I read to him from *The Philokalia*, that although we ought to say the Jesus Prayer at all times, it is especially needful to do so with the utmost care when we are preparing for Communion.

So he did, and then he made his Confession and Communion. Although from time to time the old thoughts still came over him, yet he easily drove them away with the Jesus Prayer. On Sunday, so as to be up for Mattins more easily, he went to bed earlier and went on saying the Jesus Prayer. I still sat in the corner and read my *Philokalia* by a rushlight. An hour went past; he fell asleep and I set myself to prayer. All of a sudden, about twenty minutes later, he gave a start and woke up, jumped quickly out of bed, ran over to me in tears and, speaking with the greatest happiness, he said: " Oh, brother, what I have just seen ! How peaceful and happy I am ; I believe that God has mercy upon sinners, and does not torment them. Glory to Thee, O Lord, Glory to Thee."

I was surprised and glad and asked him to tell me exactly what had happened to him.

" Why, this," he said. " Directly I fell asleep I saw myself in that meadow where they tortured me. At first I was terrified, but I saw that, instead of a cloud, the bright sun was rising and a wonderful light shining over the whole meadow. And I saw red flowers and grass in it. Then suddenly my grandfather came up to me, looking nicer than you ever saw, and he greeted me gently and kindly. And he said: ' Go to Zhitomir, to the Church of St. George. They will take you under church protection. Spend the rest of your life there and pray without ceasing. God will be gracious to you.' When he said this he made the sign of the cross over me and straight away vanished. I can't tell you how happy I felt; it was as though a load had been taken off my shoulders and I had flown away to heaven. At that point I woke up, feeling easy in my mind and my heart so full of joy that I didn't know what to do. What ought I to do now? I shall start straight away for Zhitomir, as my grandfather told me. I shall find it easy going with the Prayer.''

'' But wait a minute, dear brother. How can you start off in the middle of the night? Stay for Mattins, say your prayers and then start off with God.''

So we didn't go to sleep after this conversation. We went to church; he stayed all through Mattins, praying earnestly with tears, and he said that he felt very peaceful and glad and that the Jesus Prayer was going on happily. Then after the Liturgy he made his Communion and when we had had some food I went with him as far as the Zhitomir road, where we said good-bye with tears of gladness.

After this I began to think about my own affairs. Where should I go now? In the end I decided that I would go back again to Kiev. The wise teaching of my priest there drew me that way, and, besides, if I stayed with him he might find some Christ-loving philanthropist who would put me on my way to Jerusalem or at least to Mount Athos. So I stopped another week at Pochaev, spending the time in recalling all I had learned from those I had met on this journey and in making notes of a number of helpful things. Then I got ready for the journey, put on my *kotomka* and went to church to commend my journey to the Mother of God. When the Liturgy was over I said my prayers and was ready to start. I was standing at the back of the church when a man came in, not very richly dressed, but clearly one of the gentry, and he asked me where the candles were sold. I showed him. At the end of the Liturgy I stayed praying at the shrine of the Footprint. When I had finished my prayers I set off on my way. I had gone a little way along the street when I saw an open window in one of the houses at which a man sat reading a book. My way took me past that very window and I saw that the man sitting there was the same one who had asked me about the candles in church. As I went by I took off my hat, and when he saw me he beckoned me to come to him, and said : " I suppose you must be a pilgrim ? "

" Yes," I answered.

He asked me in and wanted to know who I was and where I was going. I told him all about myself and hid nothing. He gave me some tea and began to talk to me.

" Listen, my little pigeon ; I should advise you to go to the *Solovetsky* [12] Monastery. There is a very secluded and peaceful *skeet* [13] there called *Anzersky*. It is like a second Athos and they welcome everybody there. The novitiate consists only in this : that they take turns to read the psalter in church four hours out of the twenty-four. I am going there myself and I have taken a vow to go on foot. We might go together. I should be safer with you ; they say it is a very lonely road. On the other hand, I have got money and I could supply you with food the whole way. And I should propose we went on these terms, that we walked half a dozen yards apart ; then we should not be in each other's way, and as we went we could spend the time in reading all the while or in meditation. Think it over, brother, and do agree ; it will be worth your while."

When I heard this invitation I took this unexpected event as a sign for my journey from the Mother of God whom I had asked to teach me the way to blessedness. And without further thought I agreed at once. And so we set out the next day. We walked for three days, as we had agreed, one behind the other. He read a book the whole time, a book which never left his hand day or night ; and at times he was meditating about something. At last we came to a halt at a certain place for dinner. He ate his food with the book lying open in front of him and he was continually looking at it. I saw that the book was a copy of the Gospels, and I said to him : " May I venture to ask, sir, why you never allow the Gospels out of your hand day or night? Why you always hold it and carry it with you ? "

" Because," he answered, " from it and it alone I am almost continually learning."

" And what are you learning? " I went on.

" The Christian life, which is summed up in prayer. I consider that prayer is the most important and necessary means of salvation and the first duty of every Christian. Prayer is the first step in the devout life and also its

crown, and that is why the Gospel bids unceasing prayer.
To other acts of piety their own times are assigned, but in
the matter of prayer there are no off times. Without
prayer it is impossible to do any good and without the
Gospel you cannot learn properly about prayer. Therefore, all those who have reached salvation by way of the
interior life, the holy preachers of the Word of God, as
well as hermits and recluses, and indeed all God-fearing
Christians, were taught by their unfailing and constant
occupation with the depths of God's Word and by reading
the Gospel. Many of them had the Gospel constantly in
their hands, and in their teaching about salvation gave the
advice : ' Sit down in the silence of your cell and read
the Gospel and read it again.' There you have the reason
why I concern myself with the Gospel alone.''

I was very much pleased with this reasoning of his and
with his eagerness for prayer. I went on to ask him from
which Gospel in particular he got the teaching about
prayer. '' From all four Evangelists,'' he answered ; '' in
a word, from the whole of the New Testament, reading
it in order. I have been reading it for a long time and
taking in the meaning, and it has shown me that there is a
graduation and a regular chain of teaching about prayer
in the holy Gospel, beginning from the first Evangelist
and going right through in a regular order, in a system.
For instance, at the very beginning there is laid down the
approach, or the introduction to teaching about prayer ;
then the form or the outward expression of it in words.
Farther on we have the necessary conditions upon which
prayer may be offered, the means of learning it, and

examples ; and finally the secret teaching about interior and spiritual ceaseless prayer in the Name of Jesus Christ, which is set forth as higher and more salutary than formal prayer. And then comes its necessity, its blessed fruit, and so on. In a word, there is to be found in the Gospel full and detailed knowledge about the practice of prayer, in systematic order or sequence from beginning to end."

When I heard this I decided to ask him to show me all this in detail. So I said : " As I like hearing and talking about prayer more than anything else, I should be very glad indeed to see this secret chain of teaching about prayer in all its details. For the love of God, then, show me all this in the Gospel itself."

He readily agreed to this and said : " Open your Gospel ; look at it and make notes about what I say." And he gave me a pencil. " Be so good as to look at these notes of mine. Now," said he, " look out first of all in the Gospel of St. Matthew the sixth chapter and read from the fifth to the ninth verses. You see that here we have the preparation or the introduction, teaching that not for vainglory and noisily, but in a solitary place and in quietude, we should begin our prayer, and pray only for forgiveness of sins and for communion with God, and not devising many and unnecessary petitions about various worldly things as the heathen do. Then, read farther on in the same chapter, from the ninth to the fourteenth verses. Here the form of prayer is given to us—that is to say, in what sort of words it ought to be expressed. There you have brought together in great wisdom everything that is necessary and desirable for our life. After

that, go on and read the fourteenth and fifteenth verses of
the same chapter, and you will see the conditions it is
necessary to observe so that prayer may be effective. For
unless we forgive those who have injured us, God will not
forgive our sins. Pass on now to the seventh chapter,
and you will find in the seventh to the twelfth verses how
to succeed in prayer, to be bold in hope—ask, seek,
knock. These strong expressions depict frequency in
prayer and the urgency of practising it, so that prayer
shall not only accompany all actions but even come before
them in time. This constitutes the principal property
of prayer. You will see an example of this in the fourteenth chapter of St. Mark and the thirty-second to the
fortieth verses, where Jesus Christ Himself repeats the
same words of prayer frequently. St. Luke, chapter
eleven, verses five to fourteen, gives a similar example of
repeated prayer in the Parable of the Friend at Midnight
and the repeated request of the Importunate Widow (St.
Luke xviii. 1–8), illustrating the command of Jesus
Christ that we should pray always, at all times and in
every place, and not grow discouraged—that is to say,
not get lazy. After this detailed teaching we have shown
to us in the Gospel of St. John the essential teaching about
the secret interior prayer of the heart. In the first place
we are shown it in the profound story of the conversation
of Jesus Christ with the woman of Samaria, in which is
revealed the interior worship of God *in spirit and in truth*
which God desires and which is unceasing true prayer,
like living water flowing into eternal life (St. John iv.
5–25). Farther on, in the fifteenth chapter, verses four

to eight, there is pictured for us still more decidedly the power and the might and the necessity of inward prayer—that is to say, of the presence of the spirit in Christ in unceasing remembrance of God. Finally, read verses twenty-three to twenty-five in the sixteenth chapter of the same Evangelist. See what a mystery is revealed here. You notice that prayer in the Name of Jesus Christ, or what is known as the Jesus Prayer—that is to say, ' Lord Jesus Christ, have mercy on me '—when frequently repeated, had the greatest power and very easily opens the heart and blesses it. This is to be noticed very clearly in the case of the Apostles, who had been for a whole year disciples of Jesus Christ, and had already been taught the Lord's Prayer by Him—that is to say, ' Our Father ' (and it is through them that we know it). Yet at the end of His earthly life Jesus Christ revealed to them the mystery which was still lacking in their prayers. So that their prayer might make a definite step forward He said to them : *Hitherto have ye asked nothing in My Name. Verily I say unto you, Whatsoever ye shall ask the Father in My Name He will give it you.* And so it happened in their case. For, ever after this time, when the Apostles learned to offer prayers in the Name of Jesus Christ, how many wonderful works they performed and what abundant light was shed upon them. Now, do you see the chain, the fullness of teaching about prayer deposited with such wisdom in the Holy Gospel? And if you go on after this to the reading of the Apostolic Epistles, in them also you can find the same successive teaching about prayer.

" To continue the notes I have already given you I will show you several places which illustrate the properties of prayer. Thus, in the Acts of the Apostles the practice of it is described—that is to say, the diligent and constant exercise of prayer by the first Christians, who were enlightened by their faith in Jesus Christ (Acts iv. 31). The fruits of prayer are told us, or the results of being constantly in prayer—that is to say, the outpouring of the Holy Spirit and His gifts upon those who pray. You will see something similar to this in the sixteenth chapter, verses twenty-five and twenty-six. Then follow it up in order in the Apostolic Epistles and you will see (1) how necessary prayer is in all circumstances (Jas. v. 13–16); (2) how the Holy Spirit helps us to pray (Jude 20–21 and Rom. viii. 26); (3) how we ought all to pray in the spirit (Eph. vi. 18); (4) how necessary calm and inward peace are to prayer (Phil. iv. 6, 7); (5) how necessary it is to pray without ceasing (1 Thess. v. 17); (6) and finally we notice that one ought to pray not only for oneself but also for all men (1 Tim. ii. 1–5). Thus, by spending a long time with great care in drawing out the meaning we can find many more revelations still of secret knowledge hidden in the Word of God, which escape one if one reads it but rarely or hurriedly.

" Do you notice, after what I have now shown you, with what wisdom and how systematically the New Testament reveals the teaching of our Lord Jesus Christ on this matter which we have been tracing? In what a wonderful sequence it is put in all four Evangelists? It is like this. In St. Matthew we see the approach, the introduction to prayer, the actual form of prayer, conditions of it, and so on. Go farther. In St. Mark we find examples. In St. Luke, parables. In St. John, the secret exercise of inward prayer, although this is also found in all four Evangelists, either briefly or at length. In the Acts the practice of prayer and the results of prayer are pictured for us; in the Apostolic Epistles, and in the Apocalypse itself, many properties inseparably connected with the act of prayer. And there you have the reason that I am content with the Gospels alone as my teacher in all the ways of salvation."

All the while he was showing me this and teaching me I marked in the Gospels (in my Bible) all the places which he pointed out to me. It seemed to me most remarkable and instructive, and I thanked him very much.

Then we went on for another five days in silence. My fellow-pilgrim's feet began to hurt him very much, no doubt because he was not used to continuous walking. So he hired a cart with a pair of horses and took me with him. And so we have come into your neighbourhood and have stayed here for three days, so that when we have had some rest we can set off straight away to Anzersky, where he is so anxious to go.

The Starets. This friend of yours is splendid. Judging from his piety he must be very well instructed. I should like to see him.

The Pilgrim. We are stopping in the same place. Let me bring him to you tomorrow. It is late now. Goodbye.

54

2

THE PILGRIM. As I promised when I saw you yesterday, I have asked my revered fellow-pilgrim, who solaced my pilgrim way with spiritual conversation and whom you wanted to see, to come here with me.

The Starets. It will be very nice both for me and, I hope, also for these revered visitors of mine, to see you both and to have the advantage of hearing your experiences. I have with me here a venerable skhimnik, and here a devout priest. And so, where two or three are gathered together in the Name of Jesus Christ, there He promised to be Himself. And now, here are five of us in His Name, and so no doubt He will vouchsafe to bless us all the more bountifully. The story which your fellow pilgrim told me yesterday, dear brother, about your burning attachment to the Holy Gospel is most notable and instructive. It would be interesting to know in what way this great and blessed secret was revealed to you.

The Professor. The all-loving God, who desires that all men should be saved and come to the knowledge of the truth, revealed it to me of His great lovingkindness in a marvellous way, without any human intervention. For five years I was a professor and I led a gloomy dissipated sort of life, captivated by the vain philosophy of the world, and not according to Christ. Perhaps I should have perished altogether had I not been upheld to some extent by the fact that I lived with my very devout mother and my sister, who was a serious-minded young woman. One day, when I was taking a walk along the public boulevard, I met and made the acquaintance of an excellent young man who told me he was a Frenchman, a student who had not long ago arrived from Paris and was looking for a post as tutor. His high degree of culture delighted me very much, and he being a stranger in this country I asked him to my home and we became friends. In the course of two months he frequently came to see me. Sometimes we went for walks together and amused ourselves, and went together into company which I leave you to suppose was very immoral. At length he came to me one day with an invitation to a place of that sort ; and in order to persuade me more quickly he began to praise the particular liveliness and pleasantness of the company to which he was inviting me. After he had been speaking about it for a short while, suddenly he began to ask me to come with him out of my study where we were sitting and to sit in the drawing-room. This seemed to me very odd. So I said that I had never before noticed any reluctance on his part to be in my study, and what, I asked, was the cause of it now? And I added that the drawing-room was next door to the room where my mother and sister were, and for us to carry on this sort of conversation there would be unseemly. He pressed his point on various pretexts, and finally came out quite openly with this : " Among those books on your shelves there you have a copy of the Gospels. I have such a reverence for that book that in its presence I find a difficulty in talking about our disreputable affairs.

Please take it away from here; then we can talk freely."
In my frivolous way I smiled at his words. Taking the
Gospels from the shelf I said, "You ought to have told
me that long ago," and handed it to him, saying, "Well,
take it yourself and put it down somewhere in the room."
No sooner had I touched him with the Gospels than at
that instant he trembled and *disappeared*. This dumb-
founded me to such an extent that I fell senseless to the
floor with fright. Hearing the noise, my household came
running in to me and for a full half-hour they were unable
to bring me to my senses. In the end, when I came to
myself again, I was frightened and shaky and I felt
thoroughly upset, and my hands and my feet were
absolutely numb so that I could not move them. When
the doctor was called in he diagnosed paralysis as the
result of some great shock or fright. I was laid up for a
whole year after this, and with the most careful medical
attention from many doctors I did not get the smallest
alleviation, so that as a result of my illness it looked as
though I should have to resign my position. My mother,
who was growing old, died during this period and my
sister was preparing to take the veil, and all this increased
my illness all the more. I had but one consolation during
this time of sickness, and that was reading the Gospel,
which from the beginning of my illness never left my
hands. It was a sort of pledge of the marvellous thing
that had happened to me. One day an unknown recluse
came to see me. He was making a collection for his
monastery. He spoke to me very persuasively and told
me that I should not rely only upon medicines, which

without the help of God were unable to bring me relief, and that I should pray to God and pray diligently about this very thing, for prayer is the most powerful means of healing all sicknesses both bodily and spiritual.

" How can I pray in such a position as this, when I have not the strength to make any sort of reverence, nor can I lift my hands to cross myself? " I answered in my bewilderment. To this he said, " Well, at any rate, pray somehow." But farther he did not go, nor actually explain to me how to pray. When my visitor left me I seemed almost involuntarily to start thinking about prayer and about its power and its effects, calling to mind the instruction I had had in religious knowledge long ago when I was still a student. This occupied me very happily and renewed in my mind my knowledge of religious matters, and it warmed my heart. At the same time I began to feel a certain relief in my attack of illness. Since the book of the Gospels was continually with me, such was my faith in it as the result of the miracle ; and as I remembered also that the whole discourse upon prayer which I had heard in lectures was based upon the Gospel text, I considered that the best thing would be to make a study of prayer and Christian devotion solely upon the teaching of the Gospel. Working out its meaning, I drew upon it as from an abundant spring, and found a complete system of the life of salvation and of true interior prayer. I reverently marked all the passages on this subject, and from that time I have been trying zealously to learn this divine teaching, and with all my might, though not without difficulty, to put it into practice. While I was occupied in this way my health gradually improved, and in the end, as you see, I recovered completely. As I was still living alone I decided in thankfulness to God for His fatherly kindness, which had given me recovery of health and enlightenment of mind, to follow the example of my sister and the prompting of my own heart, and to dedicate myself to the solitary life, so that unhindered I might receive and make my own those sweet words of eternal life given me in the Word of God. So here I am at the present time, stealing off to the solitary *skeet* in the Solovetsky Monastery in the White Sea, which is called Anzersky, about which I have heard on good authority that it is a most suitable place for the contemplative life. Further I will tell you this. The Holy Gospel gives me much consolation in this journey of mine, and sheds abundant light upon my untutored mind, and warms my chilly heart. Yet the fact is that in spite of all I frankly acknowledge my weakness, and I freely admit that the conditions of fulfilling the work of devotion and attaining salvation, the requirement of thoroughgoing self-denial, of extraordinary spiritual achievements, and of most profound humility which the Gospel enjoins, frighten me by their very magnitude and in view of the weak and damaged state of my heart. So that I stand now between despair and hope. I don't know what will happen to me in the future.

The Skhimnik. With such an evident token of a special and miraculous mercy of God, and in view of your education, it would be unpardonable not only to give way to

59

depression, but even to admit into your soul a shadow of doubt about God's protection and help. Do you know what the God-enlightened Chrysostom says about this? "No one should be depressed," he teaches, "and give the false impression that the precepts of the Gospel are impossible or impracticable. God who has predestined the salvation of man has, of course, not laid commandments upon him with the intention of making him an offender because of their impracticability. No; but so that by their holiness and the necessity of them for a virtuous life they may be a blessing to us, as in this life so in eternity." Of course the regular unswerving fulfilment of God's commandments is extraordinarily difficult for our fallen nature and, therefore, salvation is not easily attained, but that same Word of God which lays down the commandments offers also the means not only for their ready fulfilment, but also comfort in the fulfilling of them. If this is hidden at first sight behind a veil of mystery, then that, of course, is in order to make us betake ourselves the more to humility, and to bring us more easily into union with God by indicating direct recourse to Him in prayer and petition for His fatherly help. It is there that the secret of salvation lies, and not in reliance upon one's own efforts.

The Pilgrim. How I should like, weak and feeble as I am, to get to know that secret, so that I might to some extent, at least, put my slothful life right, for the glory of God and my own salvation.

The Skhimnik. The secret is known to you, dear

brother, from your book, *The Philokalia*. It lies in that unceasing prayer of which you have made so resolute a study and in which you have so zealously occupied yourself and found comfort.

The Pilgrim. I fall at your feet, reverend Father. For the love of God let me hear something for my good from your lips about this saving mystery, and about holy prayer, which I long to hear about more than anything else, and about which I love reading to get strength and comfort for my very sinful soul.

The Skhimnik. I cannot satisfy your wish with my own thoughts on this exalted subject, because I have had but very little experience of it myself. But I have some very clearly written notes by a spiritual writer precisely on this subject. If the rest of those who are talking with us would like it, I will get it at once and with your permission I can read it to you all.

All. Do be so kind, reverend Father. Do not keep such saving knowledge from us.

The Secret of Salvation, Revealed by Unceasing Prayer

How is one saved? This godly question naturally arises in the mind of every Christian who realizes the injured and enfeebled nature of man, and what is left of its original urge towards truth and righteousness. Everyone who has even some degree of faith in immortality and recompense in the life to come is involuntarily faced by the thought, " How am I to be saved? " when he turns his eyes towards heaven. When he tries to find a solution of this problem, he enquires of the wise and learned. Then under their guidance he reads edifying books by spiritual writers on this subject, and sets himself unswervingly to follow out the truths and the rules he has heard and read. In all these instructions he finds constantly put before him as necessary conditions of salvation a devout life, and heroic struggles with himself which are to issue in decisive denial of self. This is to lead him on to the performance of good works, to the constant fulfilment of God's laws, and thus witness to the unshakableness and firmness of his faith. Further, they preach to him that all these conditions of salvation must necessarily be fulfilled with the deepest humility and in combination with one another. For as all good works depend one upon another, so they should support one another, complete and encourage one another, just as the rays of the sun only reveal their strength and kindle a flame when they are focused through a glass on to one point. Otherwise, *He that is unjust in the least is unjust also in much.*

In addition to this, to implant in him the strongest conviction of the necessity of this complex and unified virtue, he hears the highest praise bestowed upon the beauty of virtue, he listens to censure of the baseness and misery of vice. All this is imprinted upon his mind by truthful promises either of majestic rewards and happiness or of tormenting punishment and misery in the life to come. Such is the special character of preaching in modern times. Guided in this way, one who ardently wishes for salvation sets off in all joy to carry out what he has learned and to apply to experience all he has heard and read. But alas! even at the first step he finds it impossible to achieve his purpose. He foresees and even finds out by trial that his damaged and enfeebled nature will have the upper hand of the convictions of his mind, that his freewill is bound, that his propensities are perverted, that his spiritual strength is but weakness. He naturally goes on to the thought: Is there not to be found some kind of means which will enable him to fulfil that which the law of God requires of him, which Christian devotion demands, and which all those who have found salvation and holiness have carried out? As the result of this and in order to reconcile in himself the demands of reason and conscience with the inadequacy of his strength to fulfil them, he applies once more to the preachers of salvation with the question: How am I to be saved? How is this inability to carry out the conditions of salvation to be justified; and are those who have preached all this that he has learned themselves strong enough to carry it out unswervingly?

Ask God. Pray to God. Pray for His help.

"So would it not have been more fruitful," the enquirer concludes, "if I had, to begin with and always in every circumstance, made a study of prayer as the power to fulfil all that Christian devotion demands and by which salvation is attained?" And so he goes on to the study of prayer: he reads; he meditates; he studies the teaching of those who have written on that subject. Truly he finds in them many luminous thoughts, much deep knowledge and words of great power. One reasons beautifully about the necessity of prayer; another writes of its power, its beneficial effect—of prayer as a duty, or of the fact that it calls for zeal, attention, warmth of heart, purity of mind, reconciliation with one's enemies, humility, contrition, and the rest of the necessary conditions of prayer. But what is prayer in itself? How does one actually pray? A precise answer which can be understood by everybody to these questions, primary and most urgent as they are, is very rarely to be found, and so the ardent enquirer about prayer is again left before a veil of mystery. As a result of his general reading there is rooted in his memory an aspect of prayer which, although devout, is only external, and he arrives at the conclusion that prayer is going to church, crossing oneself, bowing, kneeling, reading psalms, *kanons* and *acathists*.[14] Generally speaking, this is the view of prayer taken by those who do not know the writings of the holy Fathers about inward prayer and contemplative action. At length, the seeker comes across the book called *Philokalia*, in which twenty-five holy Fathers set forth in an understandable way the scientific knowledge of the truth and of the essence of prayer of the heart. This begins to draw aside the veil from before the secret of salvation and of prayer. He sees that truly to pray means to direct the thought and the memory, without relaxing, to the recollection of God, to walk in His divine Presence, to awaken oneself to His love by thinking about Him, and to link the Name of God with one's breathing and the beating of one's heart. He is guided in all this by the invocation with the lips of the most Holy Name of Jesus

Christ, or by saying the Jesus Prayer at all times and in all places and during every occupation, unceasingly. These luminous truths, by enlightening the mind of the seeker and by opening up before him the way to the study and achievement of prayer, help him to go on at once to put these wise teachings into practice. Nevertheless, when he makes his attempts he is still not free from difficulty until an experienced teacher shows him (from the same book) the whole truth—that is to say, that it is prayer which is incessant which is the only effective means, alike for perfecting interior prayer and for the saving of the soul. It is frequency of prayer which is the basis, which holds together the whole system of saving activity. As Simeon the New Theologian says, " He who prays without ceasing unites all good in this one thing." So in order to set forth the truth of this revelation in all its fullness the teacher develops it in the following way :

For the salvation of the soul, first of all true faith is necessary. Holy Scripture says, *Without faith it is impossible to please God* (Heb. xi. 6). He who has not faith will be judged. But from the same Holy Scriptures one can see that man cannot himself bring to birth in him faith even as a grain of mustard seed ; that faith does not come from us, since it is the gift of God ; that faith is a spiritual gift. It is given by the Holy Spirit. That being so, what is to be done? How is one to reconcile man's need of faith with the impossibility of producing it from the human side? The way to do this is revealed in the same Holy Scriptures : *Ask, and it shall be given you.*

The Apostles could not of themselves arouse the perfection of faith within them, but they prayed to Jesus Christ, *Lord, increase our faith.* There you have an example of obtaining faith. It shows that faith is attained by prayer. For the salvation of the soul, beside true faith, good works are also required, for *Faith, if it hath not works, is dead.* For man is judged by his works and not by faith alone. *If thou wilt enter into life, keep the commandments : Do not kill ; do not commit adultery ; do not steal ; do not bear false witness ; honour thy father and mother ; love thy neighbour as thyself.* And all these commandments are required to be kept together. *For whosoever shall keep the whole law, and yet offend in one point, he is guilty of all* (Jas. ii. 10). So the Apostle James teaches. And the Apostle Paul, describing human weakness, says : *By the deeds of the law there shall no flesh be justified* (Rom. iii. 20). *For we know that the law is spiritual ; but I am carnal, sold under sin. . . . For to will is present with me, but how to perform that which is good I find not. . . . But the evil which I would not, that I do. . . . With the mind I myself serve the law of God ; but with the flesh the law of sin* (Rom. vii.). How are the required works of the law of God to be fulfilled when man is without strength, and has no power to keep the commandments? He has no possibility of doing this until he asks for it, until he prays about it. *Ye have not because ye ask not* (Jas. iv. 2) the Apostle says is the cause. And Jesus Christ Himself says : *Without Me ye can do nothing.* And on the subject of doing it with Him, He gives this teaching : *Abide in Me and I in you. He that abideth in Me and I in him, the same bringeth forth much fruit.* But to be in Him means continually to feel

His presence, continually to pray in His Name. *If ye shall ask Me anything in My Name, that will I do.* Thus the possibility of doing good works is reached by prayer itself. An example of this is seen in the Apostle Paul himself: three times he prayed for victory over temptation, bowing the knee before God the Father, that He would give him strength in the inner man, and was at last bidden above all things to pray, and to pray continually about everything.

From what has been said above, it follows that the whole salvation of man depends upon prayer, and, therefore, it is primary and necessary, for by it faith is quickened and through it all good works are performed. In a word, with prayer everything goes forward successfully; without it, no act of Christian piety can be done. Thus, the condition that it should be offered unceasingly and always belongs exclusively to prayer. For the other Christian virtues, each of them has its own time. But in the case of prayer, uninterrupted, continuous action is commanded. *Pray without ceasing.* It is right and fitting to pray always, to pray everywhere. True prayer has its conditions. It should be offered with a pure mind and heart, with burning zeal, with close attention, with fear and reverence, and with the deepest humility. But what conscientious person would not admit that he is far from fulfilling those conditions, that he offers his prayer more from necessity, more by constraint upon himself than by inclination, enjoyment and love of it? About this, too, Holy Scripture says that it is not in the power of man to keep his mind steadfast, to cleanse it from unseemly thoughts, for the *thoughts of man are evil from his youth*, and that God alone gives us another heart and a new spirit, for *both to will and to do are of God*. The Apostle Paul himself says : *My spirit (that is, my voice) prayeth, but my understanding is unfruitful* (1 Cor. xiv. 14). *We know not what we should pray for as we ought* (Rom. viii. 26), the same writer asserts. From this it follows that we in ourselves are unable to offer true prayer. We cannot in our prayers display its essential properties.

Such being the powerlessness of every human being, what remains possible for the salvation of the soul from the side of human will and strength? Man cannot acquire faith without prayer ; the same applies to good works. And, finally, even to pray purely is not within his power. What, then, is left for him to do? What scope remains for the exercise of his freedom and his strength, so that he may not perish but be saved?

Every action has its quality, and this quality God has reserved to His own will and gift. In order that the dependence of man upon God, the will of God, may be shown the more clearly, and that he may be plunged more deeply into humility, God has assigned to the will and strength of man only the *quantity* of prayer. He has commanded unceasing prayer, always to pray, at all times and in every place. By this the secret method of achieving true prayer, and at the same time faith, and the fulfilment of God's commandments, and salvation, are revealed. Thus, it is quantity which is assigned to man, as his share ; frequency of prayer is his own, and within the province of his will. This is exactly what the Fathers of the Church teach. St. Macarius the Great says truly to pray is the gift of grace. Isikhi says that frequency of prayer becomes a habit and turns into second nature, and without frequent calling upon the Name of Jesus Christ it is impossible to cleanse the heart. The Venerable Callistus and Ignatius counsel frequent, continuous prayer in the Name of Jesus Christ before all ascetic exercises and good works, because frequency brings even the imperfect prayer to perfection. Blessed Diadokh asserts that if a man calls upon the Name of God as often as possible, then he will not fall into sin. What experience and wisdom there are here, and how near to the heart these practical instructions of the Fathers are. In their experience and simplicity they throw much light upon the means of bringing the soul to perfection. What a sharp contrast with the moral instructions of the theoretical reason! Reason argues thus: Do such and such good actions, arm yourself with courage, use the strength of your will, persuade yourself by considering the happy results of virtue—*e.g.*, cleanse the mind and the heart from worldly dreams, fill their place with instructive meditations; do good and you will be respected and be at peace; live in the way that your reason and conscience require. But alas! with all its strength, all that does not attain its purpose without frequent prayer, without summoning the help of God.

Now let us go on to some further teaching of the Fathers, and we shall see what they say, *e.g.*, about purifying the soul. St. John of the Ladder writes: " When the spirit is darkened by unclean thoughts, put the enemy to flight by the Name of Jesus repeated frequently. A more powerful and effective weapon than this you will not find, in heaven or on earth." St. Gregory the Sinaite teaches thus : " Know this, that no one can control his mind by himself, and, therefore, at a time of unclean thoughts call upon the Name of Jesus Christ often and at frequent intervals, and the thoughts will quieten down." How simple and easy a method! Yet it is tested by experience. What a contrast with the counsel of the theoretical reason, which presumptuously strives to attain to purity by its own efforts.

Noting these instructions based upon the experience of the holy Fathers we pass on to the real conclusion : that the principal, the only, and a very easy method of reaching the goal of salvation and spiritual perfection is the frequency and the uninterruptedness of prayer, however feeble it may be. Christian soul, if you do not find within yourself the power to worship God in spirit and in truth, if your heart still feels no warmth and sweet satisfaction in mental and interior prayer, then bring to the sacrifice of prayer what you can, what lies within the scope of your will, what is within your power. Let the humble instrument of your lips first of all grow familiar with frequent persistent prayerful invocation. Let them call upon the mighty Name of Jesus Christ often and without interruption. This is not a great labour and is within the power of everyone. This, too, is what the precept of the Holy Apostle enjoins : *By Him, therefore, let us offer the sacrifice of praise to God continually, that is, the fruit of our lips, giving thanks to His Name* (Heb. xiii. 15).

Frequency of prayer certainly forms a habit and becomes second nature. It brings the mind and the heart into a proper state from time to time. Suppose a man continually fulfils this one commandment of God about ceaseless prayer, then in that one thing he would have fulfilled all ; for if he uninterruptedly, at all times, and in all circumstances, offers the Prayer, calling in secret upon the most holy Name of Jesus (although at first he may do so without spiritual ardour and zeal and even forcing himself), then he will have no time for vain conversation, for judging his neighbours, for useless waste of time in sinful pleasures of the senses. Every evil thought of his would meet opposition to its growth. Every sinful act he contemplated would not come to fruition so readily as with an empty mind. Much talking and vain talking would be checked or entirely done away with, and every fault at once cleansed from the soul by the gracious power of so frequently calling upon the divine Name. The frequent exercise of prayer would often recall the soul from sinful action and summon it to what is the essential exercise of its skill, to union with God. Now do you see how important and necessary quantity is in prayer? Frequency in prayer is the one method of attaining pure and true prayer. It is the very best and most effective preparation for prayer, and the surest way of reaching the goal of prayer, and salvation.

To convince yourself finally about the necessity and fruitfulness of frequent prayer, note (1) that every impulse and every thought of prayer is the work of the Holy Spirit and the voice of your guardian angel ; (2) that the

Name of Jesus Christ invoked in prayer contains in itself self-existent and self-acting salutary power, and, therefore, (3) do not be disturbed by the imperfection or dryness of your prayer, and await with patience the fruit of frequently calling upon the divine Name. Do not listen to the inexperienced, thoughtless insinuation of the vain world that lukewarm invocation, even if it be importunate, is useless repetition. No; the power of the divine Name and the frequent calling upon it will reveal its fruit in its season. A certain spiritual writer has spoken very beautifully about this. "I know," he says, "that to many so-called spiritual and wise philosophers, who search everywhere for sham greatness and practices that are noble in the eyes of reason and pride, the simple, vocal, but frequent exercise of prayer appears of little significance, as a lowly occupation, even a mere trifle. But, unhappy ones, they deceive themselves, and they forget the teaching of Jesus Christ: *Except ye be converted and become as little children, ye shall not enter into the Kingdom of Heaven* (St. Matt. xviii. 3). They work out for themselves a sort of science of prayer, on the unstable foundations of the natural reason. Do we require much learning or thought or knowledge to say with a pure heart, "Jesus, Son of God, have mercy on me"? Does not our Divine Teacher Himself praise such frequent prayer? Have not wonderful answers been received and wonderful works done by this same brief but frequent prayer? Ah, Christian soul, pluck up your courage and do not silence the unbroken invocations of your prayer, although it may be that this cry of yours comes from a heart which is still at war with itself and half filled by the world. Never mind! Only go on with it and don't let it be silenced and don't be disturbed. It will itself purify itself by repetition. Never let your memory lose hold of this: *Greater is He that is in you than he that is in the world* (1 John iv. 4). *God is greater than our heart, and knoweth all things,* says the Apostle.

And so, after all these convincing arguments that frequent prayer, so powerful in all human weakness, is certainly attainable by man and lies fully within his own will, make up your mind to try, even if only for a single day at first. Maintain a watch over yourself and make the frequency of your prayer such that far more time is occupied in the twenty-four hours with the prayerful calling upon the Name of Jesus Christ than with other matters. And this triumph of prayer over worldly affairs will in time certainly show you that this day has not been lost, but has been secured for salvation; that in the scales of the divine judgment frequent prayer outweighs your weaknesses and evil-doing and blots out the sins of that day in the memorial book of conscience; that it sets your feet upon the ladder of righteousness and gives you hope of sanctification in the life to come.[15]

The Pilgrim. With all my heart I thank you, holy Father. With that reading of yours you have given pleasure to my sinful soul. For the love of God be so kind as to allow me to copy out for myself what you have read. I can do it in an hour or two. Everything you read was so beautiful and comforting and is so understandable

and clear to my stupid mind, like *The Philokalia*, in which
the holy Fathers treat the same subject. Here, for instance, John Karpathisky in the fourth part of *The Philokalia* also says that if you have not the strength for self-
control and ascetic achievements, then know that God
is willing to save you by prayer. But how beautifully
and understandably all that is drawn out in your notebook.
I thank God first of all, and then you, that I have been
allowed to hear it.

The Professor. I also listened with great attention and
pleasure to your reading, Reverend Father. All arguments, when they rest upon strict logic, are a delight to
me. But at the same time it seems to me that they make
the possibility of continual prayer in a high degree
dependent on circumstances which are favourable to it
and upon entirely quiet solitude. For I agree that frequent and ceaseless prayer is a powerful and unique
means of obtaining the help of divine grace in all acts of
devotion for the sanctifying of the soul, and that it is
within the power of man. But this method can be used
only when man avails himself of the possibility of solitude
and quiet. In getting away from business and worries and
distractions he can pray frequently or even continually.
He then has to contend only with sloth or with the tedium
of his own thoughts. But if he is bound by duties and
by constant business, if he necessarily finds himself in a
noisy company of people, and has an earnest desire to pray
often, he cannot carry out this desire because of the
inevitable distractions. Consequently the one method of

frequent prayer, since it is dependent upon favourable circumstances, cannot be used by everybody, nor belong to all.

The Skhimnik. It is no use drawing a conclusion of that kind. Not to mention the fact that the heart which has been taught interior prayer can always pray and call upon the Name of God unhindered during any occupation, whether of the body or of the mind, and in any noise (those who know this know it from experience, and those who do not know it must be taught by gradual training), one can confidently say that no outward distraction can interrupt prayer in one who wishes to pray, for the secret thought of man does not depend upon any link with external environment and is entirely free in itself. It can at all times be perceived and directed towards prayer; even the very tongue can secretly without outward sound express prayer in the presence of many people and during external occupations. Besides, our business is surely not so important and our conversation so interesting that it is impossible during them to find a way at times of frequently calling upon the Name of Jesus Christ, even if the mind has not yet been trained to continuous prayer. Although, of course, solitude and escape from distracting things does constitute the chief condition for attentive and continuous prayer, still we ought to feel ourselves to blame for the rarity of our prayer, because the amount and frequency is under the control of everybody, both the healthy and the sick. It does lie within the scope of his will. Instances which prove this are to be found in those who, although burdened by obligations, distracting duties, cares, worries and work, have not only always called upon the divine name of Jesus Christ, but even in this way learned and attained the ceaseless inward prayer of the heart. Thus the Patriarch Photius, who was called to the patriarchal dignity from among the ranks of the senators, while governing the vast diocese of Constantinople, persevered continually in the invocation of the Name of God, and thus attained even the self-acting prayer of the heart. Thus Callistus on the holy Mount Athos learned ceaseless prayer while carrying on his busy life as a cook. So the simple-hearted Lazarus, burdened with continual work for the brotherhood, uninterruptedly, in the midst of all his noisy occupations, repeated the Jesus Prayer and was at peace. And many others similarly have practised the continuous invocation of the Name of God.

If it were an impossible thing to pray midst distracting business or in the society of other people, then, of course, it would not have been bidden us. St. John Chrysostom, in his teaching about prayer, speaks as follows: " No one should give the answer that it is impossible for a man occupied with worldly cares, and who is unable to go to church, to pray always. Everywhere, wherever you may find yourself, you can set up an altar to God in your mind by means of prayer. And so it is fitting to pray at your trade, on a journey, standing at the counter or sitting at your handicraft. Everywhere and in every place it is possible to pray, and, indeed, if a man diligently turns his attention upon himself, then everywhere he will find convenient circumstances for prayer, if only he is convinced of the fact that prayer should constitute his chief occupation and come before every other duty. And in that case he would, of course, order his affairs with greater decision ; in necessary conversation with other people he would maintain brevity, a tendency to silence, and a disinclination for useless words ; he would not be unduly anxious about worrying things. And in all these ways he would find more time for quiet prayer. In such an order of life all his actions, by the power of the invocation of the Name of God, would be signalized by success, and finally he would train himself to the uninterrupted prayerful invocation of the Name of Jesus Christ. He would come to know from experience that frequency of prayer, this sole means of salvation, is a possibility for the will of man, that it is possible to pray at all times, in all circumstances and in every place, and easily to rise from frequent vocal prayer to prayer of the mind and from that to prayer of the heart, which opens up the Kingdom of God within us.''

The Professor. I agree that during mechanical occupations it is possible and even easy to pray frequently, even continuously ; for mechanical bodily work does not require profound exercise of the mind or great consideration, and, therefore, while it is going on my mind can be immersed in continuous prayer and my lips follow in the same way. But if I have to be occupied with something exclusively intellectual, as, for instance, attentive reading, or thinking out some deep matter, or literary composition, how can I pray with my mind and my lips in such a case?

And since prayer is above all things an action of the mind, how, at one and the same time, can I give one and the same mind different sorts of things to do?

The Skhimnik. The solution of your problem is not at all difficult, if we take into consideration that people who pray continuously are divided into three classes. First, the beginners; secondly, those who have made some progress; and, thirdly, the fully trained. Now, the beginners are frequently capable of experiencing at times an impulse of the mind and heart towards God and of repeating short prayers with the lips, even while engaged in mental work. Those who have made some progress and reached a certain stability of mind are able to occupy themselves with meditation or writing in the uninterrupted presence of God as the basis of prayer. The following example will illustrate this. Imagine that a severe and exacting monarch ordered you to compose a treatise on some abstruse subject in his presence, at the steps of his throne. Although you might be absolutely occupied by your work, the presence of the king who has power over you and who holds your life in his hands would still not allow you to forget for a single moment that you are thinking, considering and writing, not in solitude, but in a place which demands of you particular reverence, respect and decorum. This lively feeling of the nearness of the king very clearly expresses the possibility of being occupied in ceaseless inward prayer even during intellectual work. So far as the others are concerned, those who by long custom or by the mercy of God have progressed from prayer of the mind and reached prayer of the heart, they do not break off their continuous prayer during profound mental exercises, nor even during sleep itself. As the All Wise has told us, *I sleep, but my heart waketh* (Cant. v. 2). Many, that is, who have achieved this mechanism of the heart acquire such an aptitude for calling upon the divine Name, that it will of itself arouse itself to prayer, incline the mind and the whole spirit to a flood of ceaseless prayer in whatever condition the one who prays finds himself, and however abstract and intellectual his occupation at the time.

The Priest. Allow me, reverend Father, to say what is in my mind. Let me have a turn and say a word or two. It was admirably put in the article you read that the one means of salvation and of reaching perfection is frequency of prayer, of whatever sort. Now, I do not very easily understand that, and it appears to me like this. What would be the use if I pray and invoke the Name of God continually with my tongue only and pay no attention to, and do not understand, what I am saying? That would be nothing but vain repetition. The result of it will only be that the tongue will go chattering on, and the mind, hindered in its meditations by this, will have its activity impaired. God does not ask for words, but for an attentive mind and a pure heart. Would it not be better to offer a prayer, be it only a short one, even rarely may be, or only at stated times, but with attention, with zeal and warmth of heart, and with due understanding? Otherwise, although you may say the prayer day and night, yet you have not got purity of mind, you are not performing a work of devotion, not achieving anything for your salvation. You are relying upon nothing but outward chatter, and you get tired and bored, and in the end the result is that your faith in prayer is completely chilled, and you throw over altogether this fruitless proceeding. Further, the uselessness of prayer with the lips only can be seen from what is revealed to us in Holy Scripture, as, for instance, *This people draweth nigh unto Me with their mouth and honoureth Me with their lips, but their heart is far from Me* (St. Matt. xv. 8). *Not everyone that saith unto Me, Lord, Lord, shall enter into the Kingdom of Heaven* (St. Matt. vii. 21). *I had rather speak five words with my understanding . . . than ten thousand words in an unknown tongue* (1 Cor. xiv. 19). All this shows the fruitlessness of outward inattentive prayer with the mouth.

The Skhimnik. There might be something in your point of view if with the advice to pray with the mouth there were not added the need for it to be continuous, if prayer in the Name of Jesus Christ did not possess self-acting power and did not win for itself attention and zeal as a result of continuity in the exercise. But as the matter now in question is frequency, length of time, and un-interruptedness of prayer (although it may be carried on at first inattentively or with dryness), then, on account of this very fact, the conclusions that you mistakenly draw come to nothing. Let us look into the matter a little more closely. One spiritual writer, after arguing the very great value and fruitfulness of frequent prayer expressed in one form of words, says finally : " Many so-called enlightened people regard this frequent offering of one and the same prayer as useless and even trifling, calling it mechanical and a thoughtless occupation of simple people. But unfortunately they do not know the secret which is revealed as a result of this mechanical exercise, they do not know how this frequent service of the lips imperceptibly becomes a genuine appeal of the heart, sinks down into the inward life, becomes a delight, becomes, as it were, natural to the soul, bringing it light and nourishment and leading it on to union with God." It seems to me that these censorious people are like those little children who were being taught the alphabet and how to read. When they got tired of it they cried out : " Would it not be a hundred times better to go fishing, like father, than to spend the whole day in ceaselessly repeating a, b, c, or scrawling on a sheet of paper with a pen ? " The value of being able to read and the enlightenment which it brings, which they could have only as a result of this wearisome learning the letters by heart, was a hidden secret to them. In the same way the simple and frequent calling upon the Name of God is a hidden secret to those people who are not persuaded of its results and its very great value. They, estimating the act of faith by the strength of their own inexperienced and short-sighted reason, forget, in so doing, that man has two natures, in direct influence one upon another, that man is made of body and soul. Why, for example, when you desire to purify your soul, do you first of all deal with your body, make it fast, deprive it of nourishment and stimulating food? It is, of course, in order that it may not hinder, or, to put it better, so that it may be the means of promoting, purity of soul and enlightenment of mind, so that the continual feeling of bodily hunger may remind you of your resolution to seek for inward perfection and the things pleasing to God, which you so easily forget. And you find by experience that through the outward fast of your body you achieve the inward refining of your mind, the peace of your heart, an instrument for the taming of your passions and a reminder of spiritual effort. And thus, by means of outward and material things, you receive inward and spiritual profit and help. You must understand the same thing about frequent prayer with the lips, which by its long duration draws out the inward prayer of the heart, and promotes union of the mind with God. It is vain to imagine that the tongue, wearied by this frequency and barren lack of understanding, will be obliged to give up entirely this outward effort of prayer as useless. No; experience here shows us exactly the opposite. Those who have practised ceaseless prayer assure us that what happens is this : One who has made up his mind to call without ceasing upon the Name of Jesus Christ or, what is the same thing, to say the Jesus Prayer continuously, at first, of course, finds difficulty and has to struggle against sloth. But the longer and the harder he works at it, the more he grows familiar with the task imperceptibly, so that in the end the lips and the tongue acquire such capacity for moving themselves that even without any effort on his part they themselves act irresistibly and say the prayer voicelessly.

At the same time the mechanism of the throat muscles is so trained that in praying he begins to feel that the saying of the prayer is a perpetual and essential property of himself, and even feels every time he stops as though something were missing in him. And so it results from this that his mind in its turn begins to yield, to listen to this involuntary action of the lips, and is aroused by it to attention which in the end becomes a source of delight to the heart, and true prayer.

There you see the true and beneficent effect of continuous or frequent vocal prayer, exactly the opposite of what people who have neither tried nor understood it suppose. Concerning those passages in Holy Scripture which you brought forward in support of your objection, these are to be explained, if we make a proper examination of them. Hypocritical worship of God with the mouth, ostentation about it, or insincere praise in the cry, "Lord, Lord," Jesus Christ exposed for this reason, that the faith of the proud Pharisees was a matter of the mouth only, and in no degree did their conscience justify their faith, nor did they acknowledge it in their heart. It was to them that these things were said, and they do not refer to saying prayers, about which Jesus Christ gave direct, explicit and definite instructions. *Men ought always to pray and not to faint.* Similarly, when the Apostle Paul says he prefers five words spoken with the understanding to a multitude of words without thought or in an unknown tongue in the Church, he is speaking about teaching in general, not about prayer in particular, on which subject he firmly says, *I will therefore that men pray every where* (1

83

Tim. ii. 8), and his is the general precept, *Pray without ceasing* (1 Thess. v. 17). Do you now see how fruitful frequent prayer is for all its simplicity, and what serious consideration the proper understanding of Holy Scripture requires?

The Pilgrim. Truly it is so, reverend Father. I have seen many who quite simply, without the light of any education whatever and not even knowing what attention is, offer the Prayer of Jesus with their mouths unceasingly. I have known them reach a stage when their lips and tongue could not be restrained from saying the prayer. It brought them such happiness and enlightenment, and changed them from weak and negligent people into *podvizhniki* and champions of virtue.[16]

The Skhimnik. Prayer brings a man to a new birth, as it were. Its power is so great that nothing, no degree of suffering will stand against it. If you like, by way of saying good-bye, brothers, I will read you a short but interesting article which I have with me.

All of them. We shall listen with the greatest pleasure.

The Skhimnik. ON THE POWER OF PRAYER

Prayer is so powerful, so mighty, that " pray, and do what you like." Prayer will guide you to right and just action. In order to please God nothing more is needed than love. " Love, and do what you will," says the blessed Augustine;[17] " for he who truly loves cannot wish to do anything which is not pleasing to the one he loves." Since prayer is the outpouring and the activity of love, then one can truly say of it similarly, " Nothing more is needed for salvation than continuous prayer." " Pray, and do what you will," and you will reach the goal of prayer. You will gain enlightenment by it.

To draw out our understanding of this matter in more detail, let us take some examples :

(1) " Pray, and think what you will," your thoughts will be purified by prayer. Prayer will give you enlightenment of mind ; it will remove and drive away all ill-judged thoughts. This is asserted by St. Gregory the Sinaite. If you wish to drive away thoughts and purify the mind his counsel is " drive them away by prayer." For nothing can control thoughts as prayer can. St. John of the Ladder also says about this : " Overcome the foes in your mind by the Name of Jesus. You will find no other weapon than this."

(2) " Pray, and do what you will." Your acts will be pleasing to God and useful and salutary to yourself. Frequent prayer, whatever it may be about, does not remain fruitless, because in it is the power of grace, *for whosoever shall call on the Name of the Lord shall be saved* (Acts ii. 21). For example : a man who had prayed without success and without devotion was granted through this prayer clearness of understanding and a call to repentance. A pleasure-loving girl prayed on her return home, and the prayer showed her the way to the virgin life and obedience to the teaching of Jesus Christ.

(3) " Pray, and do not labour much to conquer your passions by your own strength." Prayer will destroy them in you. *For greater is He that is in you than he that is in*

the world (1 John iv. 4), says Holy Scripture. And St. John Karpathisky teaches that if you have not the gift of self-control, do not be cast down, but know that God requires of you diligence in prayer and the prayer will save you. The *starets* about whom we are told in the *Otechnik* [18.] that, when he fell into sin, did not give way to depression, but betook himself to prayer and by it recovered his balance, is a case in point.

(4) " Pray, and fear nothing." Fear no misfortunes, fear no disasters. Prayer will protect you and ward them off. Remember St. Peter, who had little faith and was sinking ; St. Paul, who prayed in prison ; the monk who was delivered by prayer from the onset of temptation ; the girl who was saved from the evil purpose of a soldier as the result of prayer ; and similar cases, which illustrate the power, the might, the universality of prayer in the Name of Jesus Christ.

(5) Pray somehow or other, only pray always and be disturbed by nothing. Be gay in spirit and peaceful. Prayer will arrange everything and teach you. Remember what the saints—John Chrysostom and Mark the Podvizhnik—say about the power of prayer. The first declares that prayer, even .though it be offered by us who are full of sin, yet cleanses us at once. The latter says : " To pray somehow is within our power, but to pray purely is the gift of grace." So offer to God what it is within your power to offer. Bring to Him at first just quantity (which is within your power) and God will pour upon you strength in your weakness. " Prayer, dry and distracted may be, but continuous, will establish a habit

and become second nature and turn itself into prayer which is pure, luminous, flaming and worthy."

(6) It is to be noted, finally, that if the time of your vigilance in prayer is prolonged, then naturally no time will be left not only for doing sinful actions but even for thinking of them.

Now, do you see what profound thoughts are focused in that wise saying : " Love, and do what you will " ; " Pray, and do what you will "? How comforting and consoling is all this for the sinner overwhelmed by his weaknesses, groaning under the burden of his warring passions.

Prayer—there you have the whole of what is given to us as the universal means of salvation and of the growth of the soul into perfection. Just that. But when prayer is named, a condition is added. *Pray without ceasing* is the command of God's Word. Consequently prayer shows its most effective power and fruit when it is offered often, ceaselessly ; for frequency of prayer undoubtedly belongs to our will, just as purity, zeal and perfection in prayer are the gift of grace.

And so we will pray as often as we can ; we will consecrate our whole life to prayer, even if it be subject to distractions to begin with. Frequent practice of it will teach us attentiveness. Quantity will certainly lead on to quality. " If you want to learn to do anything whatever well you must do it as often as possible," said an experienced spiritual writer.

The Professor. Truly prayer is a great matter, and ardent frequency of it is the key to open the treasury of its grace.

But how often I find a conflict in myself between ardour and sloth. How glad I should be to find the way to gain the victory and to convince myself and arouse myself to continuous application to prayer.

The Skhimnik. Many spiritual writers offer a number of ways based upon sound reasoning for stimulating diligence in prayer. For example, (1) they advise you to steep your mind in thoughts of the necessity, the excellence, and the fruitfulness of prayer for saving the soul; (2) make yourself firmly convinced that God absolutely requires prayer of us and that His Word everywhere commands it; (3) always remember that if you are slothful and careless about prayer you can make no progress in acts of devotion nor in attaining peace and salvation, and, therefore, will inevitably suffer both punishment on earth and torment in the life to come; (4) enhearten your resolution by the example of the saints who all attained holiness and salvation by the way of continuous prayer.

Although all these methods have their value and arise from genuine understanding, yet the pleasure-loving soul which is sick with listlessness, even when it has accepted and used them, rarely sees the fruit of them, for this reason: that these medicines are bitter to its impaired sense of taste and too weak for its deeply injured nature. For what Christian is there who does not know that he ought to pray often and diligently, that God requires it of him, that we are punished for sloth in prayer, that all the saints have ardently and constantly prayed? Nevertheless, how rarely does all this knowledge show good results.

Every observer of himself sees that he justifies but little, and but rarely, these promptings of reason and conscience, and through infrequent remembrance of them lives all the while in the same bad and slothful way. And so, in their experience and godly wisdom, the holy Fathers, knowing the weakness of will and the exaggerated love of pleasure in the heart of man, take a special line about it, and in this respect put jam with the powder and smear the edge of the medicine-cup with honey. They show the easiest and most effective means of doing away with sloth and indifference in prayer, in the hope, with God's help, of attaining by prayer to perfection and the sweet expectation of love for God.

They advise you to meditate as often as possible about the state of your soul and to read attentively what the Fathers have written on the subject. They give encouraging assurance that these enjoyable inward feelings may be readily and easily attained in prayer, and say how much they are to be desired. Heartfelt delight, a flood of inward warmth and light, ineffable enthusiasm, joy, lightness of heart, profound peace and the very essence of blessedness and happy content, are all results of prayer in the heart. By steeping itself in such reflections as these, the weak cold soul is kindled and strengthened, it is encouraged by ardour for prayer, and is, as it were, enticed to put the practice of prayer to the test. As St. Isaac the Syrian says : " Joy is an enticement to the soul, joy which is the outcome of hope blossoming in the heart, and meditation upon its hope is the well-being of the heart."

The same writer continues : " At the outset of this

activity and right to the end there is presupposed some sort of method and hope for its completion, and this both arouses the mind to lay a foundation for the task and from the vision of its goal the mind borrows consolation during the labour of reaching it." In the same way St. Isikhi, after describing the hindrance that sloth is to prayer and clearing away misconceptions about the renewal of ardour for it, finally says outright : " If we are not ready to desire the silence of the heart for any other reason, then let it be for the delightful feeling of it in the soul and for the gladness that it brings." It follows from this that this Father gives the enjoyable feeling of gladness as an incitement to assiduity in prayer, and in the same way Macarius the Great teaches that our spiritual efforts (prayer) should be carried out with the purpose and in the hope of producing fruit—that is, enjoyment in our hearts. Clear instances of the potency of this method are to be seen in very many passages of *The Philokalia*, which contains detailed descriptions of the delights of prayer. One who is struggling with the infirmity of sloth or dryness in prayer ought to read them over as often as possible, considering himself, however, unworthy of these enjoyments and ever reproaching himself for negligence in prayer.

The Priest. Will not such meditation lead the inexperienced person to spiritual voluptuousness, as the theologians call that tendency of the soul which is greedy of excessive consolation and sweetness of grace, and is not content to fulfil the work of devotion from a sense of obligation and duty without dreaming about reward?

The Professor. I think that the theologians in this case are warning men against excess or greed of spiritual happiness, and are not entirely rejecting enjoyment and consolation in virtue. For if the desire for reward is not perfection, nevertheless God has not forbidden man to think about rewards and consolation, and even Himself uses the idea of reward to incite men to fulfil His commandments and to attain perfection. *Honour thy father and thy mother.* There is the command and you see the reward follows as a spur to its fulfilment, *and it shall be well with thee. If thou wilt be perfect, go, sell all that thou hast and come and follow Me.* There is the demand for perfection, and immediately upon it comes the reward as an inducement to attain perfection, *and thou shalt have treasure in heaven. Blessed are ye when men shall hate you, and when they shall separate you from their company, and shall reproach you, and cast out your name as evil, for the Son of Man's sake* (St. Luke vi. 22). There is a great demand for a spiritual achievement which needs unusual strength of soul and unshakable patience. And so for that there is a great reward and consolation, which are able to arouse and maintain this unusual strength of soul—*For your reward is great in heaven.* For this reason I think that a certain desire for enjoyment in prayer of the heart is necessary and probably constitutes the means of attaining both diligence and success in it. And so all this undoubtedly supports the practical teaching on this subject which we have just heard from the Father Skhimnik.

The Skhimnik. One of the great theologians—that is to

say, St. Macarius of Egypt—speaks in the clearest possible way about this matter. He says: "As when you are planting a vine you bestow your thought and labour with the purpose of gathering the vintage, and if you do not, all your labour will be useless, so also in prayer, if you do not look for spiritual fruit—that is, love, peace, joy and the rest—your labour will be useless. And, therefore, we ought to fulfil our spiritual duties (prayer) with the purpose and hope of gathering fruit—that is to say, comfort and enjoyment in our hearts." Do you see how clearly the holy Father answers this question about the need for enjoyment in prayer? And, as a matter of fact, there has just come into my mind a point of view which I read not long ago of a writer on spiritual things, to this effect: that the naturalness of prayer to man is the chief cause of his inclination towards it. So the examination of this naturalness, in my opinion, may also serve as a potent means of arousing diligence in prayer, the means which the Professor is so eagerly looking for.

Let me now sum up shortly some points I drew attention to in that notebook. For instance, the writer says that reason and nature lead man to the knowledge of God. The first investigates the fact that there cannot be action without cause, and ascending the ladder of tangible things from the lower to the higher, at last reaches the first Cause, God. The second displays at every step its marvellous wisdom, harmony, order, gradation, gives the basic material for the ladder which leads from finite causes to the infinite. Thus, the natural man arrives naturally at the knowledge of God.

And, therefore, there is not, and never has been, any people, any barbarous tribe, without some knowledge of God. As a result of this knowledge the most savage islander, without any impulse from outside, as it were involuntarily raises his gaze to heaven, falls on his knees, breathes out a sigh which he does not understand, necessary as it is, and has a direct feeling that there is something which draws him upwards, something urging him towards the unknown. From this foundation all natural religions arise. And in this connection it is very remarkable that universally the essence or the soul of every religion consists in secret prayer, which shows itself in some form of movement of the spirit and what is clearly an oblation, though more or less distorted by the darkness of the coarse and wild understanding of heathen people. The more surprising this fact is in the eyes of reason, the greater is the demand upon us to discover the hidden cause of this wonderful thing which finds expression in a natural movement towards prayer. The psychological answer to this is not difficult to find. The root, the head and the strength of all passions and actions in man is his innate love of self. The deep-rooted and universal idea of self-preservation clearly confirms this. Every human wish, every undertaking, every action has as its purpose the satisfaction of self-love, the seeking of the man's own happiness. The satisfaction of this demand accompanies the natural man all through his life. But the human spirit is not satisfied with anything that belongs to the senses, and the innate love of self never abates its urgency. And so desires develop more and more, the endeavour to attain happiness grows stronger, fills the imagination and incites the feelings to this same end. The flood of this inward feeling and desire as it develops is the natural arousing to prayer. It is a requirement of self-love which attains its purpose with difficulty. The less the natural man succeeds in attaining happiness and the more he has it in view, the more his longing grows and the more he finds an outlet for it in prayer. He betakes himself in petition for what he desires to the unknown Cause of all being. So it is that innate self-love, the principal element in life, is a deep-seated stimulus to prayer in the natural man. The all-wise Creator of all things has imbued the nature of man with a capacity for self-love precisely as an " enticement," to use the expression of the Fathers, which will draw the fallen being of man upwards into touch with celestial things. Oh! if man had not spoilt this capacity, if only he had kept it in its excellence, in touch with his spiritual nature! Then he would have had a powerful incentive and an effective means of bringing him along the road to moral perfection. But, alas! how often he makes of this noble capacity a base passion of self-love when he turns it into an instrument of his animal nature.

The Starets. I thank you from my heart, all my dear visitors. Your salutary conversation has been a great consolation to me and taught me, in my inexperience, many profitable things. May God give you His grace in return for your edifying love.

[They all separate.]

3

*T*HE PILGRIM. My devout friend the Professor and I could not resist our desire to start on our journey, and before doing so to look in and say a last good-bye to you and ask for your prayers.

The Professor. Yes, our intimacy with you has meant a great deal to us, and so have the salutary conversations on spiritual things which we have enjoyed at your house in company with your friends. We shall keep the memory of all this in our hearts as a pledge of fellowship and Christian love in that distant land to which we are hastening.

The Starets. Thank you for remembering me. And, by the way, how opportune your arrival is. There are two travellers stopping with me, a Moldavian monk and a hermit who has lived in silence for twenty-five years in a forest. They want to see you. I will call them at once. Here they are.

The Pilgrim. Ah, how blessed a life of solitude is! And how suitable for bringing the soul into unbroken union with God! The silent forest is like a Garden of Eden in which the delightful tree of life grows in the prayerful heart of the recluse. If I had something to live on, nothing, I think, would keep me from the life of a hermit!

The Professor. Everything seems particularly desirable to us from a distance. But we all find out by experience that every place, though it may have its advantages, has its drawbacks too. Of course, if one is melancholy by temperament, and inclined to silence, then a solitary life is a comfort. But what a lot of dangers lie along that road. The history of the ascetic life provides many instances to show that numbers of recluses and hermits, having entirely deprived themselves of human society, have fallen into self-deception and profound seductions.

The Hermit. I am surprised at how often one hears it said in Russia, not only in religious houses, but even among God-fearing lay-folk, that many who desire the hermit life, or exercise in the practice of interior prayer, are held back from following up this inclination by the fear that seductions will ruin them. Insisting on this, they bring forward instances of the conclusion their minds have arrived at as a reason alike for avoiding the interior life themselves and for keeping other people from it also. To my mind this arises from two causes : either from failure to understand the task and lack of spiritual enlightenment, or from their own indifference to contemplative achievement and jealousy lest others who are at a low level in comparison with themselves should outdistance them in this higher knowledge. It is a great pity that those who hold this conviction do not investigate the teaching of the holy Fathers on the matter, for they very decidedly teach that one ought neither to fear nor to doubt when one calls upon God. If certain of them have indeed fallen into self-deception and fanaticism, that was the result of pride, of not having a director, and of taking appearances and imagination for reality. Should such a time of testing occur, they continue, it would lead to experience and a crown of glory, for the help of God comes swiftly to protect when such a thing is permitted. Be courageous. *I am with you, fear not*, says Jesus Christ. And it follows from this that to feel fear and alarm at the interior life on the pretext of the risk of self-deception is a vain thing. For humble consciousness of one's sins, openness of soul with one's director, and " formlessness " in prayer are a strong and safe defence against those tempting illusions of which many feel so great a fear and, therefore, do not embark upon activity of the mind. Incidentally these very people find themselves exposed to temptation, as the wise words of Philotheus the Sinaite tell us. He says : " There are many monks who do not understand the illusion of their own minds, which they suffer at the hands of demons—that is to say, they give themselves diligently to only one form of activity, ' outward good works ' ; whereas of the mind—that is, of inward contemplation—they have little care, since they are unenlightened and ignorant about this." " Even if they hear of others that grace works inwardly within them, through jealousy they regard it as self-deception," St. Gregory the Sinaite declares.

The Professor. Allow me to ask you a question. Of course the consciousness of one's sins is proper for everyone who pays any attention to himself. But how does one proceed when no director is available to guide one in the way of the interior life from his own experience, and when one has opened one's heart to him, to impart to one correct and trustworthy knowledge about the spiritual life? In that case, no doubt, it would be better not to attempt contemplation rather than try it on one's own without a guide? Further: for my part, I don't readily understand how, if one puts oneself in the presence of God, it is possible to observe complete " formlessness." It is not natural, for our soul or our mind can present nothing to the imagination without form, in absolute formlessness. And why, indeed, when the mind is steeped in God, should we not present to the imagination Jesus Christ, or the Holy Trinity, and so on?

The Hermit. The guidance of a director or *starets* who is experienced and knowledgeable in spiritual things, to whom one can open one's heart every day without hindrance, with confidence and advantage, and tell one's thoughts and what one has met with on the path of interior schooling, is the chief condition for the practice of prayer of the heart by one who has entered upon the life of silence. Yet, in cases where it is impossible to find such a one, the same holy Fathers who prescribe this make an exception. Nicephorus the Monk gives clear instructions about it, thus: " During the practice of inward activity of the heart, a genuine and well-informed director is required. If such a one is not at hand, then you must diligently search for one. If you do not find him, then, calling contritely upon God for help, draw instruction and guidance from the teaching of the holy Fathers and verify it from the Word of God set forth in the Holy Scriptures." Here one must also take into consideration the fact that the seeker of goodwill and zeal can obtain something useful in the way of instruction from ordinary people also. For the holy Fathers assure us likewise, that if with faith and right intention one questions even a Saracen, he can speak words of value to us. If, on the other hand, one asks for instruction from a Prophet, without faith and a righteous purpose, then even he will not satisfy us. We see an instance of this in the case of Macarius the Great of Egypt, to whom on one occasion a simple villager gave an explanation which put an end to the distress which he was experiencing.

As regards "formlessness"—that is, not using the imagination and not accepting any sort of vision during contemplation, whether of light, or of an angel, or of Christ, or any saint, and turning aside from all dreaming —this, of course, is enjoined by experienced holy Fathers for this reason : that the power of the imagination may easily incarnate or, so to speak, give life to the representations of the mind, and thus the inexperienced might readily be attracted by these figments, take them as visions of grace, and fall into self-deception, in spite of the fact that Holy Scripture says that Satan himself may assume the form of an angel of light. And that the mind can naturally and easily be in a state of "formlessness" and keep so, even while recollecting the presence of God, can be seen from the fact that the power of the imagination can perceptibly present a thing in "formlessness" and maintain its hold upon such a presentation. Thus, for example, the representation of our souls, of the air, warmth, or cold. When you are cold you can have a lively idea of warmth in your mind, though warmth has no shape, is not an object of sight, and is not measured by the physical feeling of one who finds himself in the cold. In the same way also the presence of the spiritual and incomprehensible Being of God may be present to the mind and recognized in the heart in absolute "formlessness."

The Pilgrim. During my wanderings I have come across people, devout people, who were seeking salvation, who have told me that they were afraid to have anything to do with the interior life, and denounced it as a mere illusion. To several of them I read out of *The Philokalia* the teaching of St. Gregory the Sinaite with some profit. He says that " the action of the heart cannot be an illusion (as that of the mind can), for if the enemy desired to turn the warmth of the heart into his own uncontrolled fire, or to change the gladness of the heart into the dull pleasures of the senses, still time, experience, and the feeling itself would expose his craftiness and cunning, even for those who are not very learned." I have also met other people who, most unhappily, after knowing the way of silence and prayer of the heart, have on meeting some obstacle or sinful weakness given way to depression, and given up the inward activity of the heart which they had known.

The Professor. Yes, and that is very natural. I have myself experienced the same thing at times, on occasions when I have lapsed from the interior frame of mind or done something wrong. For since inward prayer of the heart is a holy thing, and union with God, is it not unseemly and a thing not to be dared to bring a holy thing into a sinful heart, without having first purified it by silent contrite penitence and a proper preparation for communion with God? It is better to be dumb before God than to offer Him thoughtless words out of a heart which is in darkness and distraction.

The Monk. It is a great pity that you think like that. That is despondency, which is the worst of all sins and constitutes the principal weapon of the world of darkness against us. The teaching of our experienced holy Fathers about this is quite different. Nicetas Stethatus says that if you have fallen and sunk down even into the depths of hellish evil, even then you are not to despair, but to turn quickly to God, and He will speedily raise up your fallen heart and give you more strength than you had before. So after every fall and sinful wounding of the heart the thing to do is immediately to place it in the Presence of God for healing and cleansing, just as things that have become infected, if they are exposed for some time to the power of the sun's rays, lose the sharpness and strength of their infection. Many spiritual writers speak positively about this inner conflict with the enemies of salvation, our passions. If you receive wounds a thousand times, still you should by no means give up the life-giving action—that is to say, calling upon Jesus Christ who is present in our hearts. Our actions not only ought not to turn us away from walking in the Presence of God and from inward prayer, and so produce disquiet, depression and sadness in us, but rather further our swift turning to God. The infant who is led by its mother when it begins to walk turns quickly to her and holds on to her firmly when it stumbles.

The Hermit. I look at it in this way, that the spirit of despondency, and agitating and doubting thoughts, are aroused most easily by distraction of the mind and failure to guard the silent resort of one's inner self. The ancient Fathers in their divine wisdom won the victory over despondency and received inward light and strength through hope in God, through peaceful silence and solitude, and they have given us wise and useful counsel: "sit silently in your cell and it will teach you everything."

The Professor. I have such confidence in you that I listen very gladly to your critical analysis of my thoughts about the silence which you praise so highly, and the benefits of the solitary life which hermits so love to lead. Well, this is what I think: Since all people, by the law of nature ordained by the Creator, are placed in necessary dependence upon one another and, therefore, are bound to help one another in life, to labour for one another and to be of service to one another, this sociability makes for the well-being of the human race and shows love for one's neighbour. But the silent hermit who has withdrawn from human society, in what way can he, in his inactivity, be of service to his neighbour and what contribution can he make to the well-being of human society? He completely destroys in himself that law of the Creator which concerns union in love of one's kind and beneficent influence upon the brotherhood.

The Hermit. Since this view of yours about silence is incorrect, the conclusion you draw from it will not hold good. Let us consider it in detail. (1) The man who lives in silent solitude is not only not living in a state of inactivity and idleness ; he is in the highest degree active, even more than the one who takes part in the life of society. He untiringly acts according to his highest rational nature ; he is on guard ; he ponders ; he keeps his eye upon the state and progress of his moral existence. This is the true purpose of silence. And in the measure that this ministers to his own improvement, it benefits others for whom undistracted submergence within themselves for the development of the moral life is impossible. For he who watches in silence, by communicating his inward experiences either by word (in exceptional cases) or by committing them to writing, promotes the spiritual advantage and the salvation of his brethren. And he does more, and that of a higher kind, than the private benefactor, because the private, emotional charities of people in the world are always limited by the small number of benefits conferred, whereas he who confers benefits by morally attaining to convincing and tested means of perfecting the spiritual life becomes a benefactor of whole peoples. His experience and teaching pass on from generation to generation, as we see ourselves and of which we avail ourselves from ancient times to this day. And this in no sense differs from Christian love ; it even surpasses it in its results. (2) The beneficent and most useful influence of the man who observes silence upon his neighbours is not only shown in the communication of his instructive observations upon the interior life, but also the very example of his separated life benefits the attentive layman by leading him to self-knowledge and arousing in him the feeling of reverence. The man who lives in the world, hearing of the devout recluse, or going past the door of his hermitage, feels an impulse to the devout life, has recalled to his mind what man can be upon earth, that it is possible for man to get back to that primitive contemplative state in which he issued from the hands of his Creator. The silent recluse teaches by his very silence, and by his very life he benefits, edifies and persuades to the search for God. (3) This benefit springs from genuine silence which is illuminated and sanctified by the light of grace. But if the silent one did not have these gifts of grace which make him a light to the world, even if he should have embarked upon the way of silence with the purpose of hiding himself from the society of his kind as the result of sloth and indifference, even then he would confer a great benefit upon the community in which he lives, just as the gardener cuts off dry and barren branches and clears away the weeds so that the growth of the best and most useful may be unimpeded. And this is a great deal. It is of general benefit that the silent one by his seclusion removes the temptations which would inevitably arise from his unedifying life among people and be injurious to the morals of his neighbours.

On the subject of the importance of silence, St. Isaac

the Syrian exclaims as follows : " When on one side we place all the actions of this life and on the other silence, we find that it weighs down the scales. Do not place those who perform signs and wonders in the world on a level with those who keep silence with knowledge. Love the inactivity of silence more than the satiety of greedy ones in the world and the turning of many people to God. It is better for you to cut yourself free from the bonds of sin than to liberate slaves from their servitude." Even the most elementary sages have recognized the value of silence. The philosophical school of the Neoplatonists, which embraced many adherents under the guidance of the philosopher Plotinus, developed to a high degree the inner contemplative life which is attained most especially in silence. One spiritual writer said that if the State were developed to the highest degree of education and morals, yet even then it would still be necessary to provide people for contemplation, in addition to the general activities of citizens, in order to preserve the spirit of truth, and having received it from all the centuries that are past, to keep it for the generations to come and hand it on to posterity. Such people, in the Church, are hermits, recluses and anchorites.

The Pilgrim. I think that no one has so truly valued the excellences of silence as St. John of the Ladder. " Silence," he says, " is the mother of prayer, a return from the captivity of sin, unconscious success in virtue, a continuous ascension to heaven." Yes, and Jesus Christ Himself, in order to show us the advantage and necessity of silent seclusion, often left His public preaching and went into silent places for prayer and quietude. The silent contemplatives are like pillars supporting the devotion of the Church by their secret continuous prayer. Even in the distant past one sees that many devout layfolk, and even kings and their courtiers, went to visit hermits and men who kept silence in order to ask them to pray for their strengthening and salvation. Thus the silent recluse, too, can serve his neighbour and act to the advantage and the happiness of society by his secluded prayer.

The Professor. Now, there again, that is a thought which I do not very easily understand. It is a general custom among all of us Christians to ask for each other's prayers, to want another to pray for me, and to have special confidence in a member of the Church. Is not this simply a demand of self-love? Is it not that we have only caught the habit of saying what we have heard others say, as a sort of fancy of the mind without any serious consideration? Does God require human intercession, since He foresees everything and acts according to His all-blessed Providence and not according to our desire, knowing and settling everything before our petition is made, as the Holy Gospel says? Can the prayer of many people really be any stronger to overcome His decisions than the prayer of one person? In that case God would be a respecter of persons. Can the prayer of another person really save me when everybody is commended or put to shame on the ground of his own actions? And, therefore, the request for the prayers of another person is to my mind merely a pious expression of spiritual courtesy, which shows signs of humility and a desire to please by preferring one another, and that is all.

The Monk. If one take only outward considerations into account, and with an elementary philosophy, it might be put in that way. But the spiritual reason blessed by the light of religion and trained by the experiences of the interior life goes a good deal deeper, contemplates more clearly, and in a mystery reveals something entirely different from what you have put forward. So that we may understand this more quickly and clearly, let us take an example and then verify the truth of it from the Word of God. Let us say that a pupil came to a certain teacher for instruction. His feeble capacities and, what is more, his idleness and lack of concentration prevented him from attaining any success in his studies and they put him in the category of the idle and unsuccessful. Feeling sad at this he did not know what to do, nor how to contend with his deficiencies. Then he met another pupil, a class-mate of his, who was more able than he, more diligent and successful, and he explained his trouble to him. The other took an interest in him, and invited him to work with him. " Let us work together," he said, " and we shall be keener, more cheerful and, therefore, more successful." And so they began to study together, each sharing with the other what he understood. The subject of their study was the same. And what followed after several days? The indifferent one became diligent; he came to like his work, his carelessness was changed to ardour and intelligence, which had a beneficial effect upon his character and morals also. And the intelligent one in his turn became more able and industrious. In the effect they had upon one another they arrived at a common advantage. And this is very natural, for man is born in the society of people ; he develops his rational understanding through people, habits of life, training, emotions, the action of the will—in a word, everything he receives from the example of his kind. And, therefore, as the life of men consists in the closest relations and the strongest influences of one upon another, he who lives among a certain sort of people becomes accustomed to that kind of habit, behaviour and morals. Consequently the cool become enthusiastic, the stupid become sharp, the idle are aroused to activity by a lively interest in their fellow-men. Spirit can give itself to spirit and act beneficially upon another and attract another to prayer, to attention. It can encourage him in despondency, turn him from vice, and arouse him to holy action. And so by helping each other they can become more devout, more energetic spiritually, more reverent. There you have the secret of prayer for others, which explains the devout custom on the part of Christian people of praying for one another and asking for the prayers of the brethren.

And from this one can see that it is not that God is pleased, as the great ones of this world are, by a great many petitions and intercessions, but that the very spirit and power of prayer cleanses and arouses the soul for whom the prayer is offered and presents it ready for union with God. If mutual prayer by those who are living upon earth is so beneficial, then in the same way we may infer that prayer for the departed also is mutually beneficial because of the very close link that exists between the heavenly world and this. In this way souls of the Church Militant can be drawn into union with souls of the Church Triumphant, or, what is the same thing, the living with the dead.

All that I have said is psychological reasoning, but if we open Holy Scripture we can verify the truth of it. (1) Jesus Christ says to the Apostle Peter, *I have prayed for thee, that thy faith fail not.* There you see that the power of Christ's prayer strengthens the spirit of St. Peter and encourages him when his faith is tested. (2) When the Apostle Peter was kept in prison, *prayer was made without ceasing of the church unto God for him.* Here we have revealed the help which brotherly prayer gives in the troubled circumstances of life. (3) But the clearest precept about prayer for others is put by the holy Apostle James in this way, *Confess your sins one to another, and pray for one another. . . . The effectual fervent prayer of a righteous man availeth much.* Here is definite confirmation of the psychological argument above. And what are we to say of the example of the holy Apostle Paul, which is given to us as the pattern of prayer for one another? One writer observes that this example of the holy Apostle Paul should teach us how necessary prayer for one another is, when so holy and strong a *podvizhnik* acknowledges his own need of this spiritual help. In the Epistle to the Hebrews he words his request in this way : *Pray for us : for we trust we have a good conscience, in all things willing to live honestly* (Heb. xiii.

18). When we take note of this, how unreasonable it seems to rely upon our own prayers and successes only, when a man so holy, so full of grace, in his humility asks for the prayers of his neighbours (the Hebrews) to be joined to his own. Therefore, in humility, simplicity and unity of love we should not reject or disdain the help of the prayers of even the feeblest of believers, when the clear-sighted spirit of the Apostle Paul felt no hesitation about it. He asks for the prayers of all in general, knowing that the power of God is made perfect in weakness. Consequently it can at times be made perfect in those who seem able to pray but feebly. Feeling the force of this example, we notice further that prayer one for another strengthens that unity in Christian love which is commanded by God, witnesses to humility in the spirit of him who makes the request, and, so to speak, attracts the spirit of him who prays. Mutual intercession is stimulated in this way.

The Professor. Your analysis and your proofs are admirable and exact, but it would be interesting to hear from you the actual method and form of prayer for others. For I think that if the fruitfulness and attractive power of prayer depend upon a living interest in our neighbours, and conspicuously upon the constant influence of the spirit of him who prays upon the spirit of him who asked for prayer, such a state of soul might draw one away from the uninterrupted sense of the invisible Presence of God and the outpouring of one's soul before God in one's own needs. And if one brings one's neighbour to mind just once or twice in the day, with sympathy for him, asking the help of God for him, would that not be enough for the attracting and strengthening of his soul? To put it briefly, I should like to know exactly how to pray for others.

The Monk. Prayer which is offered to God for anything whatever ought not, and cannot, take us away from the sense of the Presence of God, for if it is an offering made to God, then, of course, it must be in His Presence. So far as the method of praying for others is concerned, it must be noted that the power of this sort of prayer consists in true Christian sympathy with one's neighbour, and it has an influence upon his soul according to the extent of that sympathy. Therefore, when one happens to remember him (one's neighbour), or at the time appointed for doing so, it is well to bring a mental view of him into the Presence of God, and to offer prayer in the following form : " Most merciful God, Thy will be done, which will have all men to be saved and to come unto the knowledge of the truth, save and help Thy servant N. Take this desire of mine as a cry of love which Thou hast commanded." Commonly you will repeat those words when your soul feels moved to do so, or you might tell your beads with this prayer. I have found from experience how beneficially such a prayer acts upon him for whom it is offered.

The Professor. Your views and arguments and the edifying conversation and illuminating thoughts which spring from them are such that I shall feel bound to keep them in my memory, and to give you all the reverence and thanks of my grateful heart.

The Pilgrim and the Professor. The time has come for us to go. Most heartily we ask for your prayers upon our journey and upon our companionship.

The Starets. The God of peace that brought again from the dead our Lord Jesus, that great shepherd of the sheep, through the blood of the everlasting covenant, make you perfect in every good work to do His will, working in you that which is well pleasing in His sight, through Jesus Christ ; to whom be glory for ever and ever. Amen (Heb. xiii. 20, 21).

NOTES

[1] *Evreinov.* Literally the name means "Son of a Jew."

[2] *Kotomka.* A sort of knapsack made of birch-bark. It has two pockets, one in front and another behind, and is worn slung over the shoulder.

[3] *Starosta.* The head-man of the village community, or *Mir.*

[4] *Near the saints*—*i.e.*, near where they are buried, the Kiev-Pecherskaya Lavra. This was one of the most famous and influential monasteries in Russia and was visited by hundreds of thousands of pilgrims every year. It was founded in the eleventh century, and its catacombs still contain the uncorrupted bodies of many saints of ancient Russia.

[5] From the eighth prayer in the Morning Prayers of the Lay Prayer Book of the Russian Church.

[6] *Lavra.* Originally a monastery which followed the rule of St. Anthony, but later used simply to designate certain large monasteries. Beside Kiev, there were eight monasteries in Russia which bore the title "Lavra."

[7] *The Holy Footprint.* The legend, which is said to date from about the thirteenth century, says that Our Lady surrounded by saints appeared in a blaze of glory to a group of shepherds. The rock upon which she stood was afterwards found to bear the imprint of her foot, and from it trickled a flow of water which subsequently proved to have healing powers. A monastery was later built over the site and the shrine of the Footprint is still preserved in the crypt.

[8] *Pravoslavny.* The name which the Russians give to the Orthodox Church. Literally it means "right praising."

[9] *Raskolniki.* Literally "schismatics", sometimes, called Old Believers. In the seventeenth century Nikon, the Patriarch of Moscow, in the face of fierce opposition, carried through a reform of the Service Books. The Old Believers, led by Avvakum, seceded from the Church rather than accept the changes. The origin of Russian Dissent is, therefore, the exact opposite of the origin of English Dissent. The *Raskolniki* afterwards themselves split into more sects,

some having a priesthood and some being without. Some of these sects degenerated into oddities, and indulged in the strangest excesses. But the more sober element among the Old Believers incorporates some of the best of the Russian religious spirit and character. Altogether these sects numbered some two per cent of the Christian population of the Empire at the beginning of the twentieth century. There is an English version of the autobiography of the archpriest Avvakum.

10 *Podvizhnik.* A *podvig* is a notable exploit, and the man who performs it is a *podvizhnik.* The terms are applied in the spiritual life to outstanding achievements in the life of prayer and ascetic practices, and to those who attain to them.

11 *Bobil.* A landless peasant, hence a miserable poverty-stricken fellow.

12 *Solovetsky.* The famous monastery on the group of islands of that name in the White Sea. It was founded in 1429 by St. German and St. Sabbas. The former had been a monk of Valaam.

13 A *Skeet* is a small monastic community dependent upon a large monastery.

14 *Acathist.* One of the many forms of the liturgical hymnody of the Orthodox Church. Its characteristic is praise. There are acathists of Our Lady and of the Saints.

The *Kanon* is another element which enters into the structure of Eastern Orthodox Services. Further information on this subject may be found in the writer's article on Eastern Orthodox Services in *Liturgy and Worship*, p. 834.

15 The original has a note here as follows: "From the author's MS. received by Father Ambrose of the Dobry Monastery."

16 The original has a note here as follows: "In the nineties of the last century there died at the Troitskaya Lavra a *starets*, a layman in his hundred and eighth year; he could not read or write, but he said the Jesus Prayer even during his sleep, and lived continually as the child of God, with a heart that yearned for Him. His name was Gordi."

Troitskaya Lavra is the famous monastery of the Holy Trinity near Moscow, founded by St. Sergei in the fourteenth century. The part it played in Russian religious life has been compared by Frere in some respects to the Cluniac movement (*Links in the Chain of Russian Church History*, p. 36). The Troitskaya Lavra was intimately connected with Russian history, and was the focal point of the national movement which drove out the Poles and placed the first Romanov on the Russian throne in 1613.

[17] *St. Augustine.* The reference is to *Dilige, et quod vis fac.* St. Augustine, Tract on the First Epistle of St. John, Tract VII, Chapter X, paragraph 8, Edition Migne, III, p. 2033.

[18] *Otechnik.* Lives of the Fathers with extracts from their writings.

BIOGRAPHICAL NOTES

ANTHONY THE GREAT was born about A.D. 250 in Egypt. As a young man he adopted the solitary life of the ascetic and was perhaps the first to withdraw into the desert to live a hermit life. His influence spread widely and he kept in touch with his friend St. Athanasius the Great who wrote his *Life*.

BASIL THE GREAT. Bishop of Cæsarea in Cappadocia in the fourth century. A great writer and preacher, he was a reformer also in the spheres of the Liturgy and the monastic life. The " Liturgy of St. Basil " is used by the Orthodox on Sundays in Lent and a few other days. Orthodox monks and nuns follow the Rule of St. Basil.

BLESSED DIADOKH was Bishop of Photice in Epirus. Victor, Bishop of Utica, writing in the preface to his *History of the Barbarity of the Vandals* about the year 490, calls himself the pupil of Diadokh, and speaks in high praise of his spiritual writings. Diadokh, therefore, flourished in the second half of the fifth century. . His signature appears among those attached to the letter from the Epirote bishops to the Emperor Leo. But nothing more is known of him.

CALLISTUS THE PATRIARCH, a disciple of Gregory the Sinaite in the *skeet* of Magoola on Mount Athos, led the ascetic life for twenty-eight years in company with one Mark, and especially with Ignatius, with whom he had so great a friendship that " it appeared as though but one spirit was in the two of them." Later, after he had been made Patriarch, he was passing by Mount Athos on his way to Serbia, and during his stay in the Holy Mountain one Maxium foretold his early death. " This *starets* will not see his flock again, for behind him can be heard the funeral hymn, ' Blessed are they that are undefiled in the way.' " On his arrival in Serbia Callistus did, in fact, die. Gregory Palamas, in his treatise on the Jesus Prayer, speaks very highly of the writings of Callistus and Ignatius on the same subject. They lived in the middle of the 14th century.

CHRYSOSTOM. The most famous of the Greek Fathers. He was born about A.D. 345 at Antioch in Syria, and was trained as a lawyer. At the age of thirty-five, however, he was baptized and later ordained. He became Archbishop of Constantinople, in which office he led a life of ascetic simplicity, and was celebrated for his writings and sermons. (The name means " golden-mouthed.") He died in 407.

GREGORY THE SINAITE took the habit in the monastery on Mount Sinai about the year 1330. Later he went to Mount Athos, where he stimulated the contemplative life. He also founded three great Lavras in Macedonia, and taught the practice of unceasing prayer. Callistus, the Patriarch of Constantinople, a former pupil of his, wrote his *Life*.

ISIKHI was a native of Jerusalem and in his early years a pupil of Gregory the Theologian. He retired to one of the hermitages in Palestine for some years, but became a priest in the year 412 and established a great reputation as a teacher and interpreter of Holy Scripture. The date of his death is given as 432–433.

JOHN KARPATHISKY. Nothing certain seems to be known about this writer. But Photius speaks of reading a book which contained, beside writings of Diadokh and Nil, a section by John Karpathisky entitled, " A consoling word to the monks who have turned to him for consolation from India." This has been taken to imply that he was a contemporary of Diadokh and Nil, and belongs to the fifth century. Karpathos is an island between Rhodes and Crete, and he was presumably either a native of the island or lived there for some time.

KASSIAN THE ROMAN was born between 350 and 360, probably in the neighbourhood of Marseilles. His parents were well-known people and wealthy, and he received a good education. He went to the East and became a monk at Bethlehem. About two years later, hearing of the ascetic achievements of the Egyptian Fathers, he went with a friend, German, to visit them. This was about the year 390. Except for a short visit to their own monastery in 397, the friends stayed among the Egyptian hermits until the year 400. In that year they went to Constantinople, where they were received by St. John Chrysostom, who ordained Kassian deacon and German priest. The two friends were among those who were sent in 405 to Rome by the friends of Chrysostom to seek help for him when he was imprisoned. Kassian did not return to the East, but spent the rest of his life in his native land, still practising the severe asceticism he had learned in Egypt. He left some twelve volumes on the constitution and ordering of the monastic life, written, it is said, at the request of many in whom the monasteries he founded inspired great admiration. He died in 435 and is commemorated by the Orthodox on February 29.

MACARIUS THE GREAT (of Egypt) was the son of a peasant and himself a shepherd. Feeling a strong attraction to the hermit life, he retired to a cell near his own village and later withdrew with some other monks into the desert on the borders of Libya and Egypt. He was ordained priest and became the head of the brotherhood. He suffered at the hands of the Arians for his rigid orthodoxy, and died in the year 390 in the desert at the age of ninety, having spent sixty years in solitude. Miraculous power and the gift of prophecy were attributed to him. He left numerous writings on the spiritual life. His relics are venerated at Amalfi.

MARK THE PODVIZHNIK was one of the most notable of the Egyptian Fathers, but little is known of his life. He is said to have been mild and gentle, to have had such love of the study of Holy Scriptures that he knew both the Old and New Testaments by heart. He is supposed to have lived beyond the age of a hundred years, and to have died at the beginning of the fifth century. He left behind him the memory of his deep spirituality and of his devotion to Holy Communion ; but few of the numerous writings ascribed to him have survived.

NICETAS STETHATUS was a presbyter of the Studium in the eleventh century, and pupil of St. Simeon the New Theologian, whose virtues and wisdom he absorbed to such an extent that he was said to shine as the twin sun of his teacher.

PHILOTHEUS was *igumen* (abbot) of the Slav monastic community on Mount Sinai, but at what date is not known.

ST. JOHN OF THE LADDER, or KLIMAX, lived for forty years in a cave at the foot of Mount Sinai. Then he became Abbot of the Monastery on the Mountain. He died about 600. He wrote a book called *The Ladder to Paradise*, and from this he derives his name. *The Ladder* has been translated into English.

THEOLEPT. A monk of Mount Athos, and later Metropolitan of Philadelphia. Among his pupils at Athos was Gregory Palamas.

SOLOVETSKY
OISLE

ARKHANGEL

KAZAN

SMOLENSK
VILNA
SHKLOV
MOGILEV

MOSCOW

OREL

KIEV
ZHITOMIR
POCHAEV
BYELAYA
TSERKOV

BYELGEROD

KAMENETS PODOLSK

ODESSA

ASTRAKHAN

ENGLISH 0 100 200 300 400 500 MILES

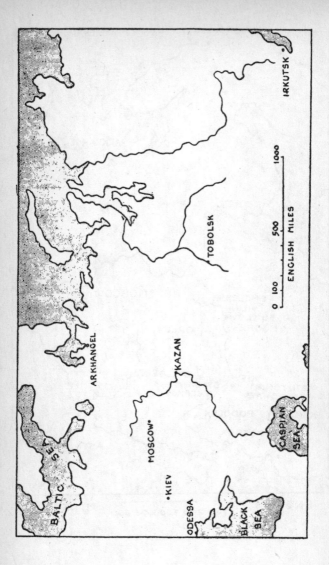